AS NEWBORN BABES

Helpful Biblical Insights For The Growing Christian

Carlton G. Christie

1 Peter 2:2

As newborn babes, desire the sincere milk of the word, that ye may grow thereby:

Presented to

From

Occasion

Place and Year

---

1 Timothy 4:12-16

12 Let no man despise thy youth; but be thou an example of the believers, in word, in conversation, in charity, in spirit, in faith, in purity.

13 Till I come, give attendance to reading, to exhortation, to doctrine.

14 Neglect not the gift that is in thee, which was given thee by prophecy, with the laying on of the hands of the presbytery.

15 Meditate upon these things; give thyself wholly to them; that thy profiting may appear to all.

16 Take heed unto thyself, and unto the doctrine; continue in them: for in doing this thou shalt both save thyself, and them that hear thee.

TABLE OF CONTENTS

INTRODUCTION

We are living in an ever changing world. The things which are common place today will be replaced by new gadgets tomorrow. Medical discoveries and technological advancements have contributed to the speed and ease with which life goes on today. It is hard to imagine how we ever got along without them. For one generation it is the worst of times while for the other it the best of times.

The older folk are quick to admit that they have certainly come a long way from steamships, horse-drawn carriages and manual type-writers. The challenge they face today is simply keeping up with faster cars, electronic devices and new technology which have taken over everyday life. Although things are quicker and easier today, and in some cases cheaper, the older generation sometimes feel like things have gotten worse — at least some things.

On the other hand, the young people have come into a world that is already advanced; a readymade paradise of sorts. Today's world, with its mp3 players, laptops, email, cellular phones, high speed internet, instant this and instant that, blogs and chat rooms, seems just perfect and is the norm for the young ones. Anything and everything seems possible now, but years ago it was not so. Changes have taken place and in some cases those changes are permanent.

Regardless of your perspective of today's world, it cannot be denied that civilization in general has advanced over the years. Yet for all the strides mankind has made in the past, hatred, strife and stress abound. What was unheard of before is not surprising nowa-days: children can take their parents to court and win; thieves can file a suit against a homeowner if they sustained injuries during an attempted home invasion; people of the same sex can marry; parents bear children for their own children; and the list goes on.

Fortunately, there is one thing that remains firm among the conflicts and paradoxes that abound in our world today; it is the immutable and sovereign Word of God, the Bible. Sadly, many do not know God or His word and find it a chore to read the Bible. Yet, it is through the Bible that God declares His will for His people and in it He shares valuable lessons concerning Himself; His love for us; and our responsibility to Him and to each other.

In this book, *As Newborn Babes*, my purpose is to share a few things with the reader directly from the Word of God (the Bible) with the hope that the reader may come to have faith in Christ Jesus and gain a good foundation as they begin and continue their Christian walk. It is hoped that with the help of the Holy Spirit the reader will understand the doctrines which are at the core of our Christian beliefs and which form the foundation of the Church of Jesus Christ.

As Newborn Babes will be a useful tool for converts to the Christian faith as they seek answers to the many questions they will have. It is also a great companion for the maturing Christians while they continue their daily walk with the Lord Jesus.

The information contained in the following pages will serve as a useful guide in your pursuit of God through His Word. Read and study it alongside your favourite version of the Bible and soon you will see that the more you read and study God's Word, the more God reveals Himself to you.

With a sound knowledge of God's Word you can resist temptations and be better equipped to lead others to the Lord Jesus Christ.

2 Timothy 2:15
Study to shew thyself approved unto God, a workman that needeth not to be ashamed, rightly dividing the word of truth.

I am sure that as you progress through this book or even after you have read it in its entirety that you may have questions of your own. It is a good idea to jot those questions down and bring them to your Bible Study group or Sunday school class. Your pastor or teacher would just love to share the answers with you.

Throughout this book you will find a number of quotations directly from the Bible. I have found it helpful as I share my faith or teach a class to let the Bible speak for itself. As such, the book is jam packed with Scriptures; sometimes a large section of a chapter is quoted.

Isaiah 8:20
To the law and to the testimony: if they speak not according to this word, it is because there is no light in them.

John 5:39
Search the scriptures; for in them ye think ye have eternal life: and they are they which testify of me.

So then, let us proceed to search the Scriptures. God has a lot to say to you through His Word, so open your heart as you open your Bible and let the Lord speak to you. But just before we do, I would also like to share two tips with you. Firstly, I have always found it helpful to pray this little Psalm each time I get ready to read my Bible.

Psalm 119:18
Open thou mine eyes, that I may behold wondrous things out of thy law.

Secondly, try to memorize as many of the Scriptures references as you possibly can. Committing the Scriptures to memory will help you as you grow to learn more of the Word of God.

Joshua 1:8
This book of the law shall not depart out of thy mouth; but thou shalt meditate therein day and night, that thou mayest observe to do according to all that is written therein: for then thou shalt make thy way prosperous, and then thou shalt have good success.

1 Timothy 4:16
Take heed unto thyself, and unto the doctrine; continue in them: for in doing this thou shalt both save thyself, and them that hear thee.

May the Lord bless you richly as you study His Word.

DEDICATION

To my family: Thanks to each of you for helping to make my life what it has become – a testimony of the goodness and the grace of God. One by one the Lord carefully placed each of you into my life and filled it with peace and purpose. I have a deep and special love for each of you.

To my parents: Papa, thanks for all the jokes you shared and the stories you told to me. I still use some of them today. Mama, thanks for all your prayers and persistence. You are not a quitter. I watched how you worked hard so that all you children could go to school and church. In a way, the readers of this book are benefiting from the investments you have made in me. Thank you ever so much.

To the reader: The quantity and quality of revelation and information available to the child of God today is phenomenal. There is absolutely no excuse for ignorance on the part of the child of God; none whatsoever. There are literally thousands of versions of Bibles, commentaries, Bible dictionaries, websites, courses, and so on. The Bible is on CD's (compact discs); the Word is also on cassettes; it is on cell phones, it is everywhere. There are downloads available on the internet from cutting edge ministries and it seems there is a preacher or church on every corner.

This book is another tool to add to the resources already available. It was written with you in mind. *As Newborn Babes* is a compilation of the lessons I have taught over the years to people who have come to me for answers. I have decided to put it all together as a memorabilia for some and a text book of sorts for others.

To those students who provided me with the notes from the lessons I taught. Thank you. In your own unique way, each of you have helped me to become a better person, a better son, better husband, a better father, a better servant, a better teacher and preacher, indeed, a better me. This is your book and mine. Indeed our book. I trust that through these pages I can share some things with you that time and schedule did not allow me to share in person. Think of it as our extended time together.

CHAPTER ONE

THE ALMIGHTY GOD, WHO IS HE?

I think it is quite appropriate to begin this study by presenting God as the first topic of discussion, just like it is found in the Scriptures. The very first verse of the Bible mentions a time, a Being, and an action. That Being is identified as God, the Creator of the heaven and the earth.

Genesis 1:1
In the beginning God created the heaven and the earth.

Notice there is no discussion on the subject of God; no telling of who He is, no introduction, no preliminaries, no commentaries. The Bible simply mentions God and expects us to believe. Why is that so? How do we know from the very onset that this God is the real God? First of all, we have been given no proof, and to make matters worse, this Bible which tells us about God was written by men He inspired to write it. Still we proceed, and the more we read the Bible, the more the God of the Bible reveals Himself to us.

As strange as it might sound, it often helps as we try to understand what we can about God, to think of how we behave as humans. How many of us would begin to tell our life's story to a total stranger? Not many of us would, unless, of course, it is a professional we go to for help, such as a counselor or doctor. But the people who stick around, those with whom we interact on a daily basis; they stand a greater chance of knowing more about us than those we casually encounter. God is no different; the more time we spend with Him, the greater the possibility of knowing more about Him.

Hosea 6:3
Then shall we know, if we follow on to know the LORD: his going forth is prepared as the morning; and he shall come unto us as the rain, as the latter and former rain unto the earth.

The Importance of Faith

God gave every man the initial faith to believe in Him. When we read that first verse in Genesis we did not throw the Book down and leave the room. Why did we bother to read on? I'll tell you why; it is because we have faith and not out of mere curiosity.

Romans 12:3
For I say, through the grace given unto me, to every man that is among you, not to think of himself more highly than he ought to think; but to think soberly, according as God hath dealt to every man the measure of faith.

God has given to every human being the measure of faith (the amount for one man) so that everyone can believe enough about God to begin to search for God. God had to do this to give mankind a fighting chance and an opportunity to choose between God and the Devil. The Scriptures tell us why:

Jeremiah 10:23
O LORD, I know that the way of man is not in himself: it is not in man that walketh to direct his steps.

Romans 8:7
Because the carnal mind is enmity against God: for it is not subject to the law of God, neither indeed can be.

Without faith it is impossible to have access to God or even please God. The Scripture teaches that we are even saved through faith.

Romans 3:22
Even the righteousness of God which is by faith of Jesus Christ unto all and upon all them that believe: for there is no difference:

Hebrews 11:6
But without faith it is impossible to please him: for he that cometh to God must believe that he is, and that he is a rewarder of them that diligently seek him.

We shall revisit the topic of Faith later on, but for now, let us turn our attention back to subject of God.

To the Unknown God

As we ponder the question of who God is, it is important that we understand that the subject of God is quite vast and any discussion around that topic is a mammoth task. God is so immeasurable that it is not possible to know everything about Him. Not to worry! Though we may not know all there is to know about God, the Bible speaks of some of His ways and other things concerning Him. It would have been impossible to know God if He did not reveal Himself to us. Rest assured, God really wants us to know Him.

Job 11:7
Canst thou by searching find out God? canst thou find out the Almighty unto perfection?

Job 36:26
Behold, God is great, and we know him not, neither can the number of his years be searched out.

The Apostle Paul encountered some men at a place called, Mars' Hill. These men had the same challenge; they were worshipping a God they did not know. So Paul took up the challenge and revealed to them what He knew about this 'unknown' God.

Acts 17:23
For as I passed by, and beheld your devotions, I found an altar with this inscription, TO THE UNKNOWN GOD. Whom therefore ye ignorantly worship, him declare I unto you.

You too should know the God you worship. Note what Jesus said to the woman of Samaria:

John 4:22-24
22 Ye worship ye know not what: we know what we worship: for salvation is of the Jews.
23 But the hour cometh, and now is, when the true worshippers shall worship the Father in spirit and in truth: for the Father seeketh such to worship him.
24 God is a Spirit: and they that worship him must worship him in spirit and in truth.

The Importance of the Word

One of the ways God reveals Himself is through the Bible, His Word.

1 Samuel 3:21
And the Lord appeared again in Shiloh: for the Lord revealed himself to Samuel in Shiloh by the word of the Lord.

John 5:39
Search the scriptures; for in them ye think ye have eternal life: and they are they which testify of me.

The Bible describes what God is like and tells of the mighty things He can do and has already done. So then, in order to know who He is, we must examine His Words and His Works.

> *Psalm 19:1*
> *The heavens declare the glory of God; and the firmament sheweth his handywork.*

It is worth repeating that spending time in the Word of God will open ones understanding to the God of the Word. So let us see what we can learn about this great, big, wonderful God.

SPECIFIC THINGS TO KNOW ABOUT GOD

God is Eternal

The first verse in the Bible highlights the fact that God was even before the beginning of the heaven and the earth. Since God created all things it means therefore that He had to have been before **all things**. Before creation there was only God. This means that God is *eternal*, that is, without beginning or end.

> *Revelation 10:6*
> *And sware by him that liveth for ever and ever, who created heaven, and the things that therein are, and the earth, and the things that therein are, and the sea, and the things which are therein, that there should be time no longer:*

> *Revelation 11:17*
> *Saying, We give thee thanks, O Lord God Almighty, which art, and wast, and art to come; because thou hast taken to thee thy great power, and hast reigned.*

The word *everlasting* means 'without ending'. Anything that was created (which is all things) cannot be classified as *eternal* because they have a beginning. However, they may fall in the category of *everlasting*.

21

Psalm 90:2
Before the mountains were brought forth, or ever thou hadst formed the earth and the world, even from everlasting to everlasting, thou art God.

Isaiah 9:6
For unto us a child is born, unto us a son is given: and the government shall be upon his shoulder: and his name shall be called Wonderful, Counsellor, The mighty God, The everlasting Father [everlasting because it was a beginning to this form of relationship], *The Prince of Peace.*

God is the Creator

One way to find out more about someone is to examine what he or she does and determine his or her function and purpose. The same is true about God; and in our first encounter with Him we discovered that He is not only alive, but active and busy as well. From Genesis 1:1 we learn that God is the Creator.

Genesis 1:1
In the beginning God created the heaven and the earth.

The Bible teaches that God created everything; from the smallest grain of sand to the tallest mountain. Everything, whether visible or invisible, tangible or intangible, present or obsolete, whether in the heaven or on the earth or under the seas, God created everything.

Genesis 2:4
These are the generations of the heavens and of the earth when they were created, in the day that the Lord God made the earth and the heavens,

Isaiah 42:5
Thus saith God the Lord, he that created the heavens, and stretched them out; he that spread forth the earth, and that

22

which cometh out of it; he that giveth breath unto the people
upon it, and spirit to them that walk therein:

John 1:3
All things were made by him; and without him was not any
thing made that was made.

What does it mean to Create?

There is a difference between the words *create* and *make*, although
at times they are used interchangeably. The basic difference is that
to *make* something one will need to use materials that are already
available. In other words, things are made from available resources.
Think about what you would need to make your favourite sandwich,
for instance, or your favorite meal. You would simply reach into
your cupboard or refrigerator and take out the necessary ingredients
and proceed to produce the meal you want. Bon Appétit!

The creation of the heavens and the earth was totally different.
God did not have any raw materials available to Him. None of the
big box hardware stores that you know were in existence. God had
to create everything from 'scratch' so to speak. He brought whatever
appeared into existence; by Himself. It never existed in any shape
or form before. He created the ingredients which He used to make
the other things.

Hebrews 11:3
Through faith we understand that the worlds were framed
by the word of God, so that things which are seen were not
made of things which do appear.

Without getting too philosophical on this topic, I wish to address
a common misconception. It is commonly taught that to *create*
means to produce something from nothing. Well, before there was
nothing, there was God. He alone fills all of time and space. God
alone then is the **Source** of all things. So, when 'nothing' was available to *make* anything, God *created* something, not 'out of nothing',

but from Himself. He then is the main ingredient in every aspect of His creation.

Colossians 1:16 & 17
16 For by him were all things created, that are in heaven, and that are in earth, visible and invisible, whether they be thrones, or dominions, or principalities, or powers: all things were created by him, and for him:
17 And he is before all things, and by him all things consist.

God is a Spirit

From Genesis 1:2 we learn about the Spirit of God:

Genesis 1:2
And the earth was without form, and void; and darkness was upon the face of the deep. And the Spirit of God moved upon the face of the waters.

A spirit is a living, intelligent and active force that is invisible to the naked eye. It goes without saying, that the Spirit of God is an active, creative, intelligent and life-giving force. In addition, anything with which the Spirit of God interacts will be made alive. No man can come in contact with God's Spirit and remain the same. No sir!

John 4:24
God is a Spirit: and they that worship him must worship him in spirit and in truth.

Romans 8:11
But if the Spirit of him that raised up Jesus from the dead dwell in you, he that raised up Christ from the dead shall also quicken your mortal bodies by his Spirit that dwelleth in you.

Please note what the following Scriptures have to say about the Spirit of God.

Job 33:4
The Spirit of God hath made me, and the breath of the Almighty hath given me life.

Romans 8:14
For as many as are led by the Spirit of God, they are the sons of God.

Ephesians 4:30
And grieve not the holy Spirit of God, whereby ye are sealed unto the day of redemption.

God is a Provider

One remarkable feature of the creation story is the fact that each day God created something that would become useful for the next day's creation. In other words, what He created on day two required the day one's creation to work effectively upon the earth. I called this the *previous day's provision theory*. It is much like what builders do; they lay one foundation and build upon it.

For instance, one of the first things God created was water. Before Genesis 1:3, where it states, "*And God said, Let there be light: and there was light*", the Bible records in Genesis 1:2 that "*darkness was upon the face of the deep. And the Spirit of God moved upon the face of the waters.*"

No civilization can survive without water, so it makes perfect sense for God to first create water if He intends for His creation to survive. Interestingly, it is also consistently displayed in Scriptures that many of God's first works usually involved water. We have already mentioned creation, but take a look at a few more examples from the brief list below.

- The first destruction of the earth

Genesis 6:17
And, behold, I, even I, do bring a flood of waters upon the earth, to destroy all flesh, wherein is the breath of life, from under heaven; and every thing that is in the earth shall die.

- The first plague in Egypt

Exodus 7:20
And Moses and Aaron did so, as the Lord commanded; and he lifted up the rod, and smote the waters that were in the river, in the sight of Pharaoh, and in the sight of his servants; and all the waters that were in the river were turned to blood.

- The first miracle that Jesus performed

John 2:9-11
9 When the ruler of the feast had tasted the water that was made wine, and knew not whence it was: (but the servants which drew the water knew;) the governor of the feast called the bridegroom,
10 And saith unto him, Every man at the beginning doth set forth good wine; and when men have well drunk, then that which is worse: but thou hast kept the good wine until now.
11 This beginning of miracles did Jesus in Cana of Galilee, and manifested forth his glory; and his disciples believed on him.

Perhaps you could add to the list just given, but I believe you get the point. Moving right along: In keeping with the concept of '*previous day's provision*', God then made light, land, plant life, aquatic life, birds, beasts, then man. Plants need water and light to survive, while the animals require the plants to survive. Man needed all of the above in order to make it on the earth.

God is the Healer

We are living in a time of tremendous technological achievements and medical advancements. Treatment and care of the sick have (in many cases) become much easier nowadays than in previous years. Although medical practitioners can provide the medicines and perform the operations, only God can heal.

Exodus 15:26
And said, If thou wilt diligently hearken to the voice of the
Lord thy God, and wilt do that which is right in his sight, and
wilt give ear to his commandments, and keep all his statutes,
I will put none of these diseases upon thee, which I have
brought upon the Egyptians: for I am the Lord that healeth
thee.

Psalm 107:20
He sent his word, and healed them, and delivered them from
their destructions.

Matthew 8:16
When the even was come, they brought unto him many that
were possessed with devils: and he cast out the spirits with
his word, and healed all that were sick:

Not only does God provide healing for our physical bodies, He provides healing for the spirit, the mind and the emotions as well. Isn't it comforting to know that God is a Healer? It seems as though the medical keys we hold are not enough to unlock the mystery of the ever increasing list of dangerous diseases that are breaking out all over the world. I don't know about you, but it sure is good to know that our God is a Healer. Hallelujah!

Psalm 103:2 & 3
2 Bless the Lord, O my soul, and forget not all his benefits:
3 Who forgiveth all thine iniquities; who healeth all thy
diseases;

Isaiah 53:5
But he was wounded for our transgressions, he was bruised for our iniquities: the chastisement of our peace was upon him; and with his stripes we are healed.

There are times however, when a loved one may succumb to his/her sickness or may have to suffer through a long illness even though they trust God as their healer. To be honest, I do not have all the answers but the Lord does; He knows how much we can bear.

2 Corinthians 12:7-9
7 And lest I should be exalted above measure through the abundance of the revelations, there was given to me a thorn in the flesh, the messenger of Satan to buffet me, lest I should be exalted above measure.
8 For this thing I besought the Lord thrice, that it might depart from me.
9 And he said unto me, My grace is sufficient for thee: for my strength is made perfect in weakness. Most gladly therefore will I rather glory in my infirmities, that the power of Christ may rest upon me.

A QUICK ASSIGNMENT

Please read the creation account found in the first chapter of Genesis and discover how God simply spoke things into being.

Psalm 33:9
For he spake, and it was done; he commanded, and it stood fast.

a) Make a list of the Days of Creation and identify the things which God created on each day.

CHAPTER TWO

THE ATTRIBUTES OF GOD

What is an Attribute?

An attribute is an inherent quality or characteristic of a person or thing that distinctly defines and describes that person or thing, and without it, that person or thing could never have existed. For example, an attribute of water is its wetness, while an attribute of fire is its heat. Water wets the immediate surface of whatever it contacts and where there is fire heat must exist. Likewise, there are some things about God that are specific to God and without them God would not be God. Here are some of the attributes of God.

God is Omnipresent

The prefix '*omni*' means, **all.** Therefore, the word '*omni*present' means to be present everywhere and at the same time. This is only true about God. Right now God is present in every country; He is in outer space and even in the depths of the sea. He is present everywhere and hears and understands everyone and everything. That is why we can pray together and it does not confuse God, because as you and/or I pray to Him, someone else in another country could be praying also, yet God still hears and answers all of us. The evil one is not everywhere. He is limited in that regard, but he has demons or fallen angels scattered all over the world.

Friend, the omnipresence of God extends to your past, present and future. He is the ever-present God; nothing can be hidden from Him.

Psalm 139:7- 12
7 Whither shall I go from thy spirit? or whither shall I flee from thy presence?
8 If I ascend up into heaven, thou art there: if I make my bed in hell, behold, thou art there.
9 If I take the wings of the morning, and dwell in the uttermost parts of the sea; 10 Even there shall thy hand lead me, and thy right hand shall hold me.
11 If I say, Surely the darkness shall cover me; even the night shall be light about me.
12 Yea, the darkness hideth not from thee; but the night shineth as the day: the darkness and the light are both alike to thee.

Proverbs 15:3
The eyes of the Lord are in every place, beholding the evil and the good.

Jeremiah 23:24
Can any hide himself in secret places that I shall not see him? saith the Lord. Do not I fill heaven and earth? saith the Lord.

God is Omnipotent

This means that God is *all-powerful* (potent) or that God has all the power. God is the mightiest, the strongest, the most powerful, the Supreme Being and He can never be defeated. He is the Almighty God.

Job 9:12
Behold, he taketh away, who can hinder him? who will say unto him, What doest thou?

Matthew 28:18
And Jesus came and spake unto them, saying, All power is given unto me in heaven and in earth.

It is vain for man to fight against God. Devils tremble at the very mention of His name. He is great and awesome, a God of power and might. Hallelujah!

Jude 25
To the only wise God our Saviour, be glory and majesty, dominion and power, both now and ever. Amen.

God is Omniscient

This means that God is *all-knowing*. He knows everything there is to know or will ever be known about everything and anything. God has perfect knowledge of everything past, present and future. God knows everything now. He will not learn anything down the road, but all that there is to know God already knows.

It is quite comforting to know that God is never surprised by anything. When we fail, and we all fail at times, we can go to Him, because He already knew we would fail and has made provisions for our restoration. God is never surprised by our actions.

Psalm 139:1-4
1 O Lord, thou hast searched me, and known me.
2 Thou knowest my downsitting and mine uprising, thou understandest my thought afar off.
3 Thou compassest my path and my lying down, and art acquainted with all my ways.
4 For there is not a word in my tongue, but, lo, O Lord, thou knowest it altogether.

Let us look closely at a couple of the verses we just read. The latter clause of verse 2 above declares that before you think a thought, God knew the thoughts you are going to think. Wow! Isn't that simply amazing! My God, You mean He is closer to me than my thoughts? It gets even better. Please read verse 4 again. God knows the words you are going to say before you say them. Our God is a wonder. Our God is awesome.

Isaiah 46:10
Declaring the end from the beginning, and from ancient times the things that are not yet done, saying, My counsel shall stand, and I will do all my pleasure:

John 16:30
Now are we sure that thou knowest all things, and needest not that any man should ask thee: by this we believe that thou camest forth from God.

God is Holy

This means that the very nature of God does not contain or condone anything sinful. As servants of God we too are required to live a life of holiness to allow us to fellowship with God.

Leviticus 20:26
And ye shall be holy unto me: for I the Lord am holy, and have severed you from other people, that ye should be mine.

Zechariah 14:20
In that day shall there be upon the bells of the horses, HOLINESS UNTO THE LORD; and the pots in the Lord's house shall be like the bowls before the altar.

Hebrews 12:14
Follow peace with all men, and holiness, without which no man shall see the Lord:

God is Just

Anything that God judges receives what it deserves. His ways are just; there is no unrighteousness with God. However, God often shows mercy in judgment, and we ought to be grateful that He does. Had He not been so merciful none of us would be alive today.

Deuteronomy 32:4
He is the Rock, his work is perfect: for all his ways are judgment: a God of truth and without iniquity, just and right is he.

Ezra 9:13
And after all that is come upon us for our evil deeds, and for our great trespass, seeing that thou our God hast punished us less than our iniquities deserve, and hast given us such deliverance as this;

Nehemiah 9:33
Howbeit thou art just in all that is brought upon us; for thou hast done right, but we have done wickedly:

Revelation 15:3
And they sing the song of Moses the servant of God, and the song of the Lamb, saying, Great and marvellous are thy works, Lord God Almighty; just and true are thy ways, thou King of saints.

There are many other attributes we could discuss. For instance, God is light. God is true. God is righteous.

God is 100 per cent of His Attributes

The 100% theory is very useful in understanding the attributes of God. It is important to note that any attribute which God possesses or anything that God is, He is 100 per cent (maximum) of that thing. It follows therefore that there is no place in Him for the opposite of that thing. For instance, if, say a water bottle is really filled to capacity, that is, it is 100 per cent filled, then there should be no empty space left in the bottle (empty being the opposite of full). The same is true about God.

Light and darkness

For example, if God is light, then He is 100 per cent light, and since that is the case, there is no place for darkness (the opposite of light) in Him. Observe how the Scripture states it:

1 John 1:5
This then is the message which we have heard of him, and declare unto you, that God is light, and in him is no darkness at all.

Truth and Lie

If we say that God is true (and He is), then, according to the theory, He is 100 per cent true. So when God speaks, His Word must be true.

John 17:17
Sanctify them through thy truth: thy word is truth.

Continuing with the theory; since God is 100 per cent true, then falsehood (the opposite of truth) cannot be found in Him. Since every word He speaks is true (John 17:17) it is therefore impossible for God to lie.

Numbers 23:19
God is not a man, that he should lie; neither the son of man, that he should repent: hath he said, and shall he not do it? or hath he spoken, and shall he not make it good?

Romans 3:4
God forbid: yea, let God be true, but every man a liar; as it is written, That thou mightest be justified in thy sayings, and mightest overcome when thou art judged.

Hebrews 6:18
That by two immutable things, in which it was impossible for
God to lie, we might have a strong consolation, who have
fled for refuge to lay hold upon the hope set before us:

Right and Wrong

Our God is a righteous God. It is His nature to do right and good things. Seeing that He is righteous; there is no unrighteousness in Him. See for yourself; He is 100 per cent righteous.

Psalm 92:15
To shew that the Lord is upright: he is my rock, and there is
no unrighteousness in him.

ANOTHER QUICK ASSIGNMENT

a) Discover some other attributes about God and measure them against the 100 % theory.
b) Make a simple chart of as many attributes of God that you can find in the Scriptures and memorize the verse describing each.

CHAPTER THREE

THE GODHEAD

The term 'Godhead' refers to the totality of God's being and power. In other words, it is the total of all that God represents. The composition of the Godhead has been the source of much controversy. In fact, there are several doctrines being taught today surrounding the number of Gods there are in the Godhead. I believe that this kind of debate is unnecessary and serves only to further divide Christian believers the world over.

The views on the Godhead may well be the one main doctrine that has not only influenced the formula for baptism but has affected the fellowship of the saints of God in many denominations around the world today. Here are three of the commonly held views.

Tritheism

This is the belief in three gods; particularly that the members of the Trinity (Father, Son and Holy Spirit) are three separate, distinct and independent beings. This is not a widespread belief among Christians, but other religions (for example Hinduism) do recognize the existence of many deities.

Trinitarianism

This is the belief in one God eternally existing in three co-equal persons. You will find this belief being expressed on the websites belonging to many Christian ministries. Those who adhere to this belief often describe the godhead like an equilateral triangle which being one shape, but comprising three equal angles.

Monotheism

This is the belief in one God. The Hebrew people in Bible days believed in one God. He was known by various names which we shall look into later on, but they all knew Him to be the same One Lord God.

Deuteronomy 6:4
Hear, O Israel: The Lord our God is one Lord:

Isaiah 43:15
I am the LORD, your Holy One, the creator of Israel, your King.

The Only Thing the Devil and I Agree On

Satan, the accuser of the brethren (Revelation 12:10), is called by many other names in the Scriptures. In this book I refer to him as the evil one. Whatever you call him he is still the same deceptive, enemy of our soul whose main desire is to steal, kill and destroy (John 10:10). Strangely, the devil and I agree on one thing, that is, there is one God.

Luke 4:34
Saying, Let us alone; what have we to do with thee, thou Jesus of Nazareth? art thou come to destroy us? I know thee who thou art; the Holy One of God.

James 2:19
Thou believest that there is one God; thou doest well: the devils also believe, and tremble.

Jesus Taught the Oneness of God

In the Scriptures below, Jesus made it clear that there is only one God; and that He is not divided.

Matthew 19:17
And he said unto him, Why callest thou me good? there is none good but one, that is, God: but if thou wilt enter into life, keep the commandments.

Matthew 23:8-10
8 But be not ye called Rabbi: for one is your Master, even Christ; and all ye are brethren.
9 And call no man your father upon the earth: for one is your Father, which is in heaven.
10 Neither be ye called masters: for one is your Master, even Christ.

What does it mean to be One?

Firstly, '*one*' means a single unit. That is, apart from God there is no other God. This is what God said about Himself through the Scriptures.

Isaiah 43:10
Ye are my witnesses, saith the Lord, and my servant whom I have chosen: that ye may know and believe me, and understand that I am he: before me there was no God formed, neither shall there be after me.

Zechariah 14:9
And the Lord shall be king over all the earth: in that day shall there be one Lord, and his name one.

Secondly, '*one*' also means He is whole. He is not a fraction, but the whole, He is One. A fraction requires another fraction to make it one, but God is already One. Thus He is complete in Himself and requires nothing or no one outside of Himself to make Him complete. This is such a marvelous revelation: that God is complete in Himself, wanting nothing. Things which humans find essential to their survival do not move God at all. God will still be God without any of those things. Let us look at two of them.

God and Food

Take food for example. We all need food; and lots of it too. Especially if it is one of those home cooked meals that we all love so much. But God does not need to eat. He is self-sustaining, the All-Sufficient One, the El-Shaddai (Genesis 17:1) and requires nothing outside of Himself.

Psalm 50:12-14
12 If I were hungry, I would not tell thee: for the world is mine, and the fulness thereof.
13 Will I eat the flesh of bulls, or drink the blood of goats?
14 Offer unto God thanksgiving; and pay thy vows unto the most High:

God and Sleep

How about sleep? Too much sleep is not good either. In the book of Proverbs, Solomon gave some warnings against too much sleep.

Proverbs 6:9-11
9 How long wilt thou sleep, O sluggard? when wilt thou arise out of thy sleep?
10 Yet a little sleep, a little slumber, a little folding of the hands to sleep:
11 So shall thy poverty come as one that travelleth, and thy want as an armed man.

Proverbs 20:13
Love not sleep, lest thou come to poverty; open thine eyes,
and thou shalt be satisfied with bread.

But not having enough sleep is not good either. Soldiers use sleep deprivation to torture prisoners of war. Although those in the medical arena disagree on exactly how many hours we should sleep per day, they all agree that an adequate amount of sleep is a good and healthy thing. However, God does not sleep.

Psalm 121:4-5
4 Behold, he that keepeth Israel shall neither slumber nor
sleep.
5 The LORD is thy keeper: the LORD is thy shade upon thy
right hand.

Baal and Sleep

In one of my favourite passages of the Scriptures, the prophet Elijah taunted the prophets of a false god called Baal, as they tried in vain to get Baal to respond to their cry. You should read the entire story (fantastic reading) but in the verse below Elijah all but pointed out that, unlike our God, Baal could be taking a nap.

1 Kings 18:27
And it came to pass at noon, that Elijah mocked them, and
said, Cry aloud: for he is a god; either he is talking, or he is
pursuing, or he is in a journey, or peradventure he sleepeth,
and must be awaked.

The Manifestations of God

There have been some confusion surrounding the Godhead and much of it had to do with the *manifestations* of God or the ways God reveals Himself to mankind. In these revelations God assumes certain roles, the three main ones being as the Father, as the Son and as the Holy Ghost. These are roles or manifestations and should not be viewed as separate Gods. Remember, there is only one God.

Matthew 28:19
Go ye therefore, and teach all nations, baptizing them in the
name of the Father, and of the Son, and of the Holy Ghost:

Remember what I said about sometimes thinking about how we are as humans when we think about God? Well, once again, if we take a moment to think about ourselves we will soon realize that individually we also assume roles, but still remain one person. We just wear a lot of different hats; that's all. Take me for instance; I am a father, a son and a husband, yet I am one person. God can become whatever He wants to become, but never ceases to be who He is. He is the One Lord God. He can manifest Himself in any shape or form but never ceases to be who He is.

Exodus 13:21
And the LORD went before them by day in a pillar of a cloud,
to lead them the way; and by night in a pillar of fire, to give
them light; to go by day and night:

Being God provides Him with options. He can do whatever He wants to, whenever He wants to. He is a Sovereign God! So if He so chooses, He can manifest Himself in as many forms as He so pleases. But, friend, these are just forms; He is still the One Lord God. Amen.

The Three Forms of Water

Take water as another example. Water can exist in three different states; frozen (*ice*), liquid (*water*) or vapor (*steam*); but remains water nonetheless. It should not surprise you that God can become whatever He wants to become but never stops being who He is; and He is God. Besides, seeing as He is God, then nothing is impossible to Him.

Mark 10:27
And Jesus looking upon them saith, With men it is impossible,
but not with God: for with God all things are possible.

So whether God is fulfilling the role of the Father, the Son, or the Holy Ghost, He is still just one God.

Philippians 2:6-7
6 Who, being in the form of God, thought it not robbery to be
equal with God:
7 But made himself of no reputation, and took upon him the
form of a servant, and was made in the likeness of men:

God is the Father in/of Creation

The term 'Father' is used many times in the Scriptures in reference to God and underscores the fact that He is the Creator, Originator, Progenitor and Source of all things. In other words, He is the Father in [relation to] creation, and of creation, as the following Scripture states.

Revelation 4:11
Thou art worthy, O Lord, to receive glory and honour and
power: for thou hast created all things, and for thy pleasure
they are and were created.

The Lord is the best example of a Father there is. Not only is He the Source of our existence, but He also takes the best care of His own. You see, to father does not only mean to source biologically, but it also means to take care of, to provide for and to protect. Many men today perform the role of a father in the lives of children who are not their biological offspring.

Psalm 136:25
Who giveth food to all flesh: for his mercy endureth for
ever.

43

Matthew 5:45
That ye may be the children of your Father which is in heaven: for he maketh his sun to rise on the evil and on the good, and sendeth rain on the just and on the unjust.

Matthew 6:28-30
28 And why take ye thought for raiment? Consider the lilies of the field, how they grow; they toil not, neither do they spin:
29 And yet I say unto you, That even Solomon in all his glory was not arrayed like one of these.
30 Wherefore, if God so clothe the grass of the field, which to day is, and to morrow is cast into the oven, shall he not much more clothe you, O ye of little faith?

By looking at some of the things mentioned above, we conclude that our God is a loving and caring God who heals, delivers and provides for His entire creation.

God is the Son in Redemption

In this role, God, who is a spirit (John 4:24) assumes the role of a human being. Jesus is the embodiment of God in the flesh (John 1:14) for the purpose of redemption.

2 Corinthians 5:19
To wit, that God was in Christ, reconciling the world unto himself, not imputing their trespasses unto them; and hath committed unto us the word of reconciliation.

In the Jewish society, the son plays a vital role. He takes over in the absence of his father, provides for the family and carries on the family name. So it is with Jesus, the Son of God. He represents God upon the earth and when we assume His name we have the name of the Heavenly family.

Ephesians 3:14 & 15
14 For this cause I bow my knees unto the Father of our Lord Jesus Christ,
15 Of whom the whole family in heaven and earth is named,

Jesus' filial nature was also foreshadowed in the lives of other Bible characters. For example, like Joseph, He was loved of His of Father and hated of His brethren. Like Isaac, He was the humble and submissive sacrifice of the Father. The Scripture references are below:

Genesis 37:4
And when his brethren saw that their father loved him more than all his brethren, they hated him, and could not speak peaceably unto him.

Genesis 22:9
And they came to the place which God had told him of; and Abraham built an altar there, and laid the wood in order, and bound Isaac his son, and laid him on the altar upon the wood.

Since the Son is God (Hebrews 1:8), then it should not surprise you that Jesus is both the Lamb of God and the Good Shepherd (who sacrifices the Lamb). He is both Shepherd and Sheep. God is versatile. He can do anything.

John 1:29
The next day John seeth Jesus coming unto him, and saith, Behold the Lamb of God, which taketh away the sin of the world.

John 10:11
I am the good shepherd: the good shepherd giveth his life for the sheep.

God is the Holy Ghost in the Church

The Holy Spirit is a comforter and guide, much like a husband is to his wife.

> *John 14:16-18*
> *16 And I will pray the Father, and he shall give you another Comforter, that he may abide with you for ever;*
> *17 Even the Spirit of truth; whom the world cannot receive, because it seeth him not, neither knoweth him: but ye know him; for he dwelleth with you, and shall be in you.*
> *18 I will not leave you comfortless: I will come to you.*

In the last verse (vs. 18) above, Jesus, God in the flesh, advised the disciples that he will come back as the Comforter. Did you miss it? Note, he said, I will come to you. Of course, the Scriptures must confirm this:

> *1 Corinthians 15:45*
> *And so it is written, The first man Adam was made a living soul; the last Adam was made a quickening spirit.*

> *2 Corinthians 3:17*
> *Now the Lord is that Spirit: and where the Spirit of the Lord is, there is liberty.*

I have reserved more discussion on this manifestation of the one God for later on in this book. When we are done you will understand what *role* the Son and the Holy Ghost play in the whole plan of salvation.

The Father and the Son

The father-son phenomenon should not be too much of a surprise because that combination is all around us today. For instance, I am a father and a son, too. How? I'm glad you asked. Well, God blessed me and my wife to produce three lovely children. That made me a father (praise God); and the fact that I am here today proves that I am my parents' son.

Similarly, the Father and the Son are one. Do not take my word for it either. Here is what the Bible says.

Isaiah 9:6
For unto us a child is born, unto us a son is given: and the government shall be upon his shoulder: and his name shall be called Wonderful, Counseller, The mighty God, The everlasting Father, The Prince of Peace.

John 14:8 & 9
8 Philip saith unto him, Lord, shew us the Father, and it sufficeth us.
9 Jesus saith unto him, Have I been so long time with you, and yet hast thou not known me, Philip? he that hath seen me hath seen the Father; and how sayest thou then, Shew us the Father?

John 10:30
I and my Father are one.

ANOTHER QUICK ASSIGNMENT

Think about the roles you fill being just one person and discuss with your teacher how those roles help you to understand the manifestations of God.

CHAPTER FOUR

WHAT IS GOD'S NAME?

A spiritual being takes its name from the function it is performing at the time and will respond to that name when it is used during the execution of the assigned function. Since God is a Spirit, and He performs many functions and He goes by various names in the Bible.

Genesis 17:1
And when Abram was ninety years old and nine, the Lord appeared to Abram, and said unto him, I am the Almighty God; walk before me, and be thou perfect.

Exodus 3:14
And God said unto Moses, I AM THAT I AM: and he said, Thus shalt thou say unto the children of Israel, I AM hath sent me unto you.

Exodus 6:3
And I appeared unto Abraham, unto Isaac, and unto Jacob, by the name of God Almighty, but by my name Jehovah was I not known to them.

Exodus 34:14
For thou shalt worship no other god: for the Lord, whose name is Jealous, is a jealous God:

Isaiah 9:6
For unto us a child is born, unto us a son is given: and the government shall be upon his shoulder: and his name shall be called Wonderful, Counsellor, The mighty God, The everlasting Father, The Prince of Peace.

Matthew 1:21
And she shall bring forth a son, and thou shalt call his name Jesus: for he shall save his people from their sins.

Matthew 1:23
Behold, a virgin shall be with child, and shall bring forth a son, and they shall call his name Emmanuel, which being interpreted is, God with us.

The Function is in the Name

Each of the names mentioned above was given or used at a time when God assumed a specific function, and so, the name declares the function. For example, in Matthew 1:21 above, God chose the name *Jesus* to underline the fact that He is fulfilling the role of a Saviour, for the name 'Jesus' means, 'Jehovah became my salvation'.

Matthew 1:21
And she shall bring forth a son, and thou shalt call his name Jesus: [and why that name?] *for he shall save his people from their sins.*

Compound Names of God

There are several compound Hebrew names of God given in the Scriptures. Here are some of them.

Genesis 22:14
And Abraham called the name of that place Jehovah-jireh: as it is said to this day, In the mount of the Lord it shall be seen.

Exodus 17:15
And Moses built an altar, and called the name of it Jehovah-nissi:

Judges 6:24
Then Gideon built an altar there unto the Lord, and called it Jehovah-shalom: unto this day it is yet in Ophrah of the Abi-ezrites.

Ezekiel 48:35
It was round about eighteen thousand measures: and the name of the city from that day shall be, The Lord is there. Jehovah-shammah

Jeremiah 23:6
In his days Judah shall be saved, and Israel shall dwell safely: and this is his name whereby he shall be called, THE LORD OUR RIGHTEOUSNESS. Jehovah-tsidkenu

What's in a Name?

We have already established that spiritual beings respond to the name that describes their function. That is why it is necessary to know the name of God because He is a Spirit (John 4:24) and He will respond to His name. The wonderful thing about the name of Jesus is that it contains all the functions of the individual names of God. That means we no longer need to know a specific name that is aligned with a specific function. All we need to know is the name Jesus. Hallelujah!

The Name of Jesus Grants us Audience

This is why we pray in the name of Jesus; the name which guarantees that our prayers will be heard.

John 14:13 & 14
13 And whatsoever ye shall ask in my name, that will I do,
that the Father may be glorified in the Son.
14 If ye shall ask any thing in my name, I will

There is Deliverance in the Name of Jesus

God will supply whatever we need when we get His attention by calling on His name. He is able to heal us from any sickness and deliver us out of any situation. He is the God of the mountain and the God in the valley. He works around the clock and is always on duty.

Joel 2:32
And it shall come to pass, that whosoever shall call on the
name of the LORD shall be delivered: for in mount Zion and
in Jerusalem shall be deliverance, as the LORD hath said,
and in the remnant whom the LORD shall call.

There is Healing in the Name of Jesus

Jesus authorized His disciples to use His name when ministering to the sick. Note what He told them in the Scripture below.

Mark 16:17-18
17 And these signs shall follow them that believe; In my
name shall they cast out devils; they shall speak with new
tongues;
18.They shall take up serpents; and if they drink any deadly
thing, it shall not hurt them; they shall lay hands on the sick,
and they shall recover.

Therefore, after His departure, the apostles continued to use the mighty name of Jesus to bring healing and deliverance.

Acts 3:6
Then Peter said, Silver and gold have I none; but such as I have give I thee: In the name of Jesus Christ of Nazareth rise up and walk.

There is Authority in the Name of Jesus

The name of Jesus carries the authority and power of heaven. A police officer today can command and remand when he operates in the name of the law. The name of Jesus gives the believer the same authority in the spirit realm.

Mark 16:17
And these signs shall follow them that believe; In my name shall they cast out devils; they shall speak with new tongues;

Peter and John stood as Jesus' representatives when they used His name and so they had *audience* with God and received *authority* to *heal* and to *deliver*. You and I ought to use the name of Jesus. The Scriptures give us more reasons to do so.

Ephesians 3:14 & 15
14 For this cause I bow my knees unto the Father of our Lord Jesus Christ,
15 Of whom the whole family in heaven and earth is named,

Colossians 3:17
And whatsoever ye do in word or deed, do all in the name of the Lord Jesus, giving thanks to God and the Father by him.

Philippians 2:9-11
9 Wherefore God also hath highly exalted him, and given him a name which is above every name:
10 That at the name of Jesus every knee should bow, of things in heaven, and things in earth, and things under the earth;
11 And that every tongue should confess that Jesus Christ is Lord, to the glory of God the Father.

The Scripture says 'whatsoever' we do should be done in Jesus' name. Friend that is why we preach in Jesus' name; teach in Jesus' name; pray in Jesus' name; witness in Jesus' name; and baptize in Jesus' name! Beloved, the name of Jesus is so powerful that countless numbers of tyrants have tried but failed to erase it off the face of the earth.

Acts 5:40-42
40 And to him they agreed: and when they had called the apostles, and beaten them, they commanded that they should not speak in the name of Jesus, and let them go.
41And they departed from the presence of the council, rejoicing that they were counted worthy to suffer shame for his name.
42And daily in the temple, and in every house, they ceased not to teach and preach Jesus Christ.

1 Peter 4:14
If ye be reproached for the name of Christ, happy are ye; for the spirit of glory and of God resteth upon you: on their part he is evil spoken of, but on your part he is glorified.

ANOTHER QUICK ASSIGNMENT

a) Find out what each of the five compound names mentioned means.
b) There are other compound names of God. You should ask your Bible teacher to help you discover the others and their meanings.

CHAPTER FIVE

WHAT IS MAN?

According to the Genesis account, God began His creative acts on the first day and finished on the sixth day. During that time God created everything; but His final creation was man.

Genesis 1:27
So God created man in his own image, in the image of God created he him; male and female created he them.

Man is God's prized creation and is the only 'thing' which God created in His own image and likeness. The Lord saw a reflection of Himself each time He saw the man which He created. I believe God created man in order to fulfill His own word and works. I'll explain.

During the creation period the Lord God commanded the living things which He created to be fruitful and multiply and to produce after their kind. God also set an example by also producing after His kind. So He made man in His own image and after His own likeness.

Genesis 2:7
And the LORD God formed man of the dust of the ground, and breathed into his nostrils the breath of life; and man became a living soul.

You may have noticed that man was both created and made. The Bible says that man was created in the likeness and image of God yet his natural *body* was made from the dust of the earth. Afterwards God *breathed* into the body and man became alive [*a living soul*].

Composition of Man

God used the dust of the ground to make a body. Then He breathed (His Spirit) into man so that man could become a living soul. Mankind therefore is a spirit; he has a soul, and lives in a body. Man is a trichotomy.

1 Thessalonians 5:23
And the very God of peace sanctify you wholly; and I pray God your whole spirit and soul and body be preserved blameless unto the coming of our Lord Jesus Christ.

With the Spirit Mankind has God Consciousness

There is inherent in every man an innate desire to worship a supreme power. This 'unknown God' (to some) deserves and desires worship. We worship God in and by our spirit.

Romans 1:9
For God is my witness, whom I serve with my spirit in the gospel of his Son, that without ceasing I make mention of you always in my prayers;

Sadly, many have tried to satisfy this thirst for God with strange religions and philosophies, but Jesus, the only true and living God, is the answer for every seeking, longing soul. He only can satisfy the soul of man.

Acts 17:23-28
23 For as I passed by, and beheld your devotions, I found an altar with this inscription, TO THE UNKNOWN GOD.

Whom therefore ye ignorantly worship, him declare I unto you.
24 God that made the world and all things therein, seeing that he is Lord of heaven and earth, dwelleth not in temples made with hands;
25 Neither is worshipped with men's hands, as though he needed any thing, seeing he giveth to all life, and breath, and all things;
26 And hath made of one blood all nations of men for to dwell on all the face of the earth, and hath determined the times before appointed, and the bounds of their habitation;
27 That they should seek the Lord, if haply they might feel after him, and find him, though he be not far from every one of us:
28 For in him we live, and move, and have our being; as certain also of your own poets have said, For we are also his offspring.

With the Soul Mankind has Self-Consciousness

The soul makes man aware of who he is. He knows he is not a dog or any other animal, but that he is a human being. He knows how to operate and how to socialize. It is the soul of man that contains the emotions. Through the soul we gain the use of our five senses, which are, seeing, smelling, hearing, tasting and feeling. Sometimes in Scripture the word 'soul' is used interchangeably with 'person'.

Acts 2:41
Then they that gladly received his word were baptized: and the same day there were added unto them about three thousand souls.

The soul is the most important part of the human being and is the total of the individual. To lose ones soul is to lose everything. Dear reader, your soul is precious.

Matthew 16:26
For what is a man profited, if he shall gain the whole world,
and lose his own soul? or what shall a man give in exchange
for his soul?

Your body may be sick, but if it is well with your soul, then there
is not much about which to worry.

Psalm 124:7
Our soul is escaped as a bird out of the snare of the fowlers:
the snare is broken, and we are escaped.

3 John 1:2
Beloved, I wish above all things that thou mayest prosper
and be in health, even as thy soul prospereth.

With the Body the Individual has World Consciousness

This means that the person can feel and respond to the world
around him. For instance, he or she can tell whether it is hot or cold.
When an individual dies, the body goes back to the ground [*from*
whence it came] and the individual ceases to exist in the world in
bodily form. As a result, the individual can no longer respond to
anything in the world.

Genesis 3:19
In the sweat of thy face shalt thou eat bread, till thou return
unto the ground; for out of it wast thou taken: for dust thou
art, and unto dust shalt thou return.

Psalm 115:17
The dead praise not the Lord, neither any that go down into
silence.

Though we can only reach out to God through our spirit, yet it
needs the platform of the body to do so. We have to experience life

as humans, in order to reach out to the divine God in the spirit. That is why it is essential to seek for God when we are alive. Why?

Psalm 6:5
For in death there is no remembrance of thee: in the grave who shall give thee thanks?

Hebrews 9:27
And as it is appointed unto men once to die, but after this the judgment:

The Development of Man

It is quite interesting to see how God went about developing the man He created. However, before we look at the first Adam perhaps it would help if we took a look at Jesus, the last Adam (1 Corinthians 15:45).

Jesus learnt or developed by His experiences with the things that were placed in His responsibility. There are also some lessons you and I will learn from the things we go through. Amen.

Hebrews 5:8
Though he were a Son, yet learned he obedience by the things which he suffered;

Luke 2:52
And Jesus increased in wisdom and stature, and in favour with God and man.

This verse in Luke 2:52 above is very important because it tells of the areas in which Jesus (the last Adam) developed. He developed in wisdom (intellectually), stature (physically), with God (spiritually) and with man (socially).

Let us now go back to the first Adam. How did Adam develop intellectually, physically, spiritually and socially? Well God is going to develop Adam by his experiences, much in the same Jesus also developed.

Intellectual Development

Adam developed intellectually when he named 'every living creature' and kept the commandment of God.

Genesis 2:16 & 17, 19 & 20
16 And the Lord God commanded the man, saying, Of every tree of the garden thou mayest freely eat:
17 But of the tree of the knowledge of good and evil, thou shalt not eat of it: for in the day that thou eatest thereof thou shalt surely die.

19 And out of the ground the Lord God formed every beast of the field, and every fowl of the air; and brought them unto Adam to see what he would call them: and whatsoever Adam called every living creature, that was the name thereof.
20 And Adam gave names to all cattle, and to the fowl of the air, and to every beast of the field; but for Adam there was not found an help meet for him.

Physical Development

Adam developed physically when he maintained (worked) the Garden of Eden. Work still works and the first thing God gave man was a job.

Genesis 2:15
And the Lord God took the man, and put him into the Garden of Eden to dress it and to keep it.

Spiritual Development

Adam developed spiritually by communing with God. God wants us to grow in grace and in faith. Wishing for it will not make it happen. There is no magic formula. It is simply a daily diet of prayer and the Word. The Word of God will help you to please God and overcome temptation. Let's get back to the Bible shall we!

Genesis 3:8
And they heard the voice of the Lord God walking in the garden in the cool of the day: and Adam and his wife hid themselves from the presence of the Lord God amongst the trees of the garden.

Social Development

Adam developed socially because God gave him a wife in Eve. We do not have much of a problem with socializing today, but there is still room for improvement when it comes to spending quality time with our children, our family and our spouses.

Genesis 2:18, 21-24
18 And the Lord God said, It is not good that the man should be alone; I will make him an help meet for him.

21 And the Lord God caused a deep sleep to fall upon Adam and he slept: and he took one of his ribs, and closed up the flesh instead thereof;
22 And the rib, which the Lord God had taken from man, made he a woman, and brought her unto the man.
23 And Adam said, This is now bone of my bones, and flesh of my flesh: she shall be called Woman, because she was taken out of Man.
24 Therefore shall a man leave his father and his mother, and shall cleave unto his wife: and they shall be one flesh.

Before God created man He made provision for His survival. In other words, everything that man would need was already provided before man came onto the scene. We shall see in the pages to follow that the evil one, Satan, realized that the only way to affect God was to interfere with mankind - the object of God's love. It is still a puzzle (even for mankind himself) to understand why God loves mankind so much. Observe what the psalmist David said.

Psalm 8:4 & 5
4 What is man, that thou art mindful of him? and the son of man, that thou visitest him?
5 For thou hast made him a little lower than the angels, and hast crowned him with glory and honour.

CHAPTER SIX

YIELD NOT TO TEMPTATION

The intention of the evil one is to bring man into contention with God. So he tempts us to do things that will cause us to violate the Word and will of God. Living outside the Word and will of God can bring destruction to an individual and cause the ungodly man to lose his soul. So what then is a temptation?

Definition

A temptation can be described as the enticement or desire to satisfy a legitimate need in a sinful way. Sometimes temptation comes from an external source. For example the devil used food to tempt Jesus in the wilderness (St. Matthew 4) and Eve in the Garden of Eden (Genesis 3).

However, there are times when temptation comes from our own desire. Remember that Lucifer had no tempter; he sinned on his own accord.

James 1:14 & 15
14 But every man is tempted, when he is drawn away of his own lust, and enticed.
15 Then when lust hath conceived, it bringeth forth sin: and sin, when it is finished, bringeth forth death.

Does God Tempt Anyone?

From the definition given above the answer right away would be 'No'. But let us examine the Scriptures some more.

James 1:13
Let no man say when he is tempted, I am tempted of God:
for God cannot be tempted with evil, neither tempteth he any
man:

Earlier we read that we learn or develop by our experiences, and in order to have a strong spiritual defense system it must be tested and evaluated by our resistance to temptation. Similarly, it is customary in the school system that the teacher gives a test to assess how well the students are learning. God allows tests to come our way in order to build our faith and show us where we are most vulnerable.

God and evil

It should be made clear, however, that even though God allows temptations to come our way He personally does not tempt anyone with evil. Think about it keeping in mind the 100 % theory of God's attributes. In order for God to tempt you with evil He would have to think of evil and such a feat is impossible for God because (anything God is, He is that thing 100 percent, and since He is good there can be no evil in God) the Lord is good.

Psalms 34:8
O taste and see that the LORD is good: blessed is the man
that trusteth in him.

Psalms 100:5
For the LORD is good; his mercy is everlasting; and his
truth endureth to all generations.

Psalms 135:3
Praise the LORD; for the LORD is good: sing praises unto his name; for it is pleasant.

Psalms 145:9
The LORD is good to all: and his tender mercies are over all his works.

Jeremiah 33:11
The voice of joy, and the voice of gladness, the voice of the bridegroom, and the voice of the bride, the voice of them that shall say, Praise the LORD of hosts: for the LORD is good; for his mercy endureth for ever: and of them that shall bring the sacrifice of praise into the house of the LORD. For I will cause to return the captivity of the land, as at the first, saith the LORD.

Lamentations 3:25
The LORD is good unto them that wait for him, to the soul that seeketh him.

Nahum 1:7
The LORD is good, a strong hold in the day of trouble; and he knoweth them that trust in him.

It would be unfair of God to tempt us with evil and then punish us if we fail. In addition, if we were to overcome the temptation it would appear that we were more righteous than God. How impossible is that! How then can a good God use evil to tempt anyone? The word to watch there is evil. It goes against all of God's attributes if He were to tempt anyone to sin; God wants us to do right, not wrong.

Jeremiah 29:11
For I know the thoughts that I think toward you, saith the Lord, thoughts of peace, and not of evil, to give you an expected end.

Test versus Temptation

In the King James Version of the Bible, sometimes the word 'tempt' is used instead of 'test', as in the case of Abraham (Genesis 22:1-12).

Genesis 22:1
And it came to pass after these things, that God did tempt Abraham, and said unto him, Abraham: and he said, Behold, here I am.

The Hebrew word translated as *tempt* in the verse above really means, to prove or try. God was trying Abraham's faith.

James 1:3
Knowing this, that the trying of your faith worketh patience.

In life we face tests all the time; which are designed to prove to us whether or not we grasped a lesson or a particular principle that we have been taught. Notice I said, "to us". They are not proof for God because God knows everything. He is omniscient. The tests that God allows into our lives are designed to make us aware of our strengths, weaknesses and our limitations. That way, we know who, what, and where to avoid.

Exodus 20:20
And Moses said unto the people, Fear not: for God is come to prove you, and that his fear may be before your faces, that ye sin not.

The Difference between a Test and a Temptation

There is a difference between a test and a temptation. Here are some things to remember:

1. God may test us, but He also allows temptations.
2. The aim of the test is to build your faith, but the goal of temptation is to cause you to sin.
3. If you fail a test you simply get another chance at it until you pass, but when you yield to temptation it means you have sinned.

Whatever you may be going through right now is a test; learn the lessons well and pass your test. God wants to take you to the next level in Him. Your faith is tested, but when you are tempted, it is always to do evil.

Your Temptation is not Unique

It is typical of the evil one to at times, make you feel like you are the only one facing a certain temptation. If he succeeds in causing you to feel that way then you may be tempted to keep it a secret, fearing that no one will understand or be in position to help. Rest assured, your temptation is not unique and there is a way that you can overcome it.

1 Corinthians 10:13
There hath no temptation taken you but such as is common to man: but God is faithful, who will not suffer you to be tempted above that ye are able; but will with the temptation also make a way to escape, that ye may be able to bear it.

The Scripture above is saying that temptation is common. Someone else was tempted in the same way you are being tempted; you can draw on someone else's experience, whether in life or from the Bible. That is one reason why God never hides from us the failures of the people that He uses.

Romans 15:4
For whatsoever things were written aforetime were written for our learning, that we through patience and comfort of the scriptures might have hope.

Being Tempted is not a Sin

Here is another ploy of the evil one. He will try to play on your feelings by making you feel guilty for being tempted in a certain way. Friend, sin is committed only when you yield to the temptation. If being tempted was a sin then the Scriptures declaring Jesus' sinless life would be false.

Hebrews 4:15
For we have not an high priest which cannot be touched with the feeling of our infirmities; ***but was in all points tempted like as we are, yet without sin.***

If being tempted was a sin, Jesus would be a sinner. Because being tempted does not constitute sin, Jesus *knew no sin, did no sin,* and had no sin.

2 Corinthians 5:21
For he hath made him to be sin for us, who knew no sin; that we might be made the righteousness of God in him.

1 Peter 2:22
Who did no sin, neither was guile found in his mouth:

1 John 3:5
And ye know that he was manifested to take away our sins; and in him is no sin

Temptations usually come in the Form of a Need

An effective temptation will come in the form of a need. Boast not that you have overcome it if the source of your temptation was never a true and real need. Curiosity does pose a threat at times and in many cases it gets the better of the best of us. Curiosity aside, only a real need can be an effective source of temptation. Think about it, who is more likely to be tempted to smoke, a non-smoker or an ex-smoker? Most likely, the ex-smoker. The non-smoker may be curious, but the ex-smoker's body would remember the nicotine of the past.

Why did the evil one tempt Eve with a fruit and tempt Jesus to turn stones into bread? The simple answer is, that food, in both cases, were legitimate needs. Eve had a need for beauty and wisdom, but both Eve and Jesus were hungry. Here's what the Bible said:

Genesis 3:6
And when the woman saw that the tree was good for food, and that it was pleasant to the eyes, and a tree to be desired to make one wise, she took of the fruit thereof, and did eat, and gave also unto her husband with her; and he did eat.

Matthew 4:2-3
2 And when he had fasted forty days and forty nights, he was afterward an hungred.
3 And when the tempter came to him, he said, If thou be the Son of God, command that these stones be made bread.

Temptation has an Inner Ally

What is waved before our eyes is only half of the temptation. The other half is the seed that is being planted by our senses, that is, what we see, hear, smell, taste and feel as we are exposed to the temptation. It is this inner desire and need which intensifies the battle our temptation. This is precisely what the Scripture says:

James 1:14
But every man is tempted, when he is drawn away of his own lust, and enticed.

The Apostle Paul called this inner pull, a law (Romans 7:21-24). Our challenge fellow brethren, is to win the battle on the inside. This is crucial because the outer temptation is seeking to connect with an inner ally or desire in order to cause you to sin.

Jesus, was not under that law at all, and could proclaim:

John 14:30
Hereafter I will not talk much with you: for the prince of this world cometh, and hath nothing in me.

The Wheat and Tares

Someone once said the constant dripping of water can dig a hole in a rock. How true! In other words, a seemingly harmless practice can become quite harmful over a period of time. The evil one is cunning and he will try to plant seeds in your heart and life any way he can. At first, these seeds may appear quite harmless, but they will affect you when they are grown and usually when you least expect it.

Matthew 13:24-30
24 Another parable put he forth unto them, saying, The kingdom of heaven is likened unto a man which sowed good seed in his field:
25 But while men slept, his enemy came and sowed tares among the wheat, and went his way.
26 But when the blade was sprung up, and brought forth fruit, then appeared the tares also.
27 So the servants of the householder came and said unto him, Sir, didst not thou sow good seed in thy field? from whence then hath it tares?
28 He said unto them, An enemy hath done this. The servants said unto him, Wilt thou then that we go and gather them up?
29 But he said, Nay; lest while ye gather up the tares, ye root up also the wheat with them.
30 Let both grow together until the harvest: and in the time of harvest I will say to the reapers, Gather ye together first the tares, and bind them in bundles to burn them: but gather the wheat into my barn.

A Lesson from Samson

The point to note in the story of Samson is that the constant exposure to sin can make one vulnerable. Samson learned this lesson the hard way. In the sixteenth chapter of the book of Judges we find that Samson was entertaining Delilah's advances until one day he went too far and succumbed to them.

> *Judges 16:20*
> *And she said, The Philistines be upon thee, Samson. And he awoke out of his sleep, and said, I will go out as at other times before, and shake myself. And he wist not that the LORD was departed from him.*

How many times have you come across an obnoxious scene in an otherwise good movie or book? Something which made you blushed. Perhaps if you knew it were there you would have avoided it or at least not watched or read it in public. It is odd how some things are included when it was totally unnecessary. Friend, that is the evil one actively and desperately planting seeds in the heart and mind. It is no surprise that the evils which are now main stream in our world today were subtly introduced a little at a time in our schools, music, books, and movies before they become blatant.

I can Overcome Temptation

The Scripture we read in 1 Corinthians 10:13 also underscores the fact that God is faithful, 100 % faithful. Praise God! You can trust God enough to know that He will never allow a temptation into your life that is going to prove too difficult for you to bear. He will (without fail) make a way of escape for you so that may be victorious in it. Hallelujah!

> *1 John 4:4*
> *Ye are of God, little children, and have overcome them: because greater is he that is in you, than he that is in the world.*

However, not everybody takes the escape route that God has provided. Joseph was able to run away from the advances of Potiphar's wife, but Samson chose not to get away from Delilah. We, too, have a choice to make.

Genesis 39:12
And she caught him by his garment, saying, Lie with me: and he left his garment in her hand, and fled, and got him out.

CHAPTER SEVEN

HOW TO OVERCOME TEMPTATION

With each victory over temptation, the child of God becomes stronger and stronger and moves on from faith to faith. Rest assured however, that the devil will present you with other temptations at each new level that you climb in God. Nevertheless, our God has provided valuable tools with which to secure the victory and when all else fails, God Himself will help us.

Zechariah 4:6
Then he answered and spake unto me, saying, This is the word of the Lord unto Zerubbabel, saying, Not by might, nor by power, but by my spirit, saith the Lord of hosts.

Jude 1:24
Now unto him that is able to keep you from falling, and to present you faultless before the presence of his glory with exceeding joy,

God is able to keep you through each temptation but most times our failure is due to the fact that we did not follow his Word. The following are just a few of the tools God has given us to help us overcome temptations.

Use the Word of God - "It is written"

Using Jesus' example (St. Matthew 4:1-11 & St. Luke 4:1-13) we see that one of the most effective tools against temptations is the Word of God. It is not good enough just to know the Word, you should understand the benefits lie in applying it rightfully.

John 7:17
If any man will do his will, he shall know of the doctrine, whether it be of God, or whether I speak of myself.

2 Timothy 2:15
Study to shew thyself approved unto God, a workman that needeth not to be ashamed, rightly dividing the word of truth.

James 1:22
But be ye doers of the word, and not hearers only, deceiving your own selves.

It is in the Word of God that we find out what God expects of us. With that knowledge we can avoid those things that displease God.

Psalm 119:9
Wherewithal shall a young man cleanse his way? by taking heed thereto according to thy word.

Psalm 119:11
Thy word have I hid in mine heart, that I might not sin against thee.

Psalm 119:104
Through thy precepts I get understanding: therefore I hate every false way.

Micah 6:8
He hath shewed thee, O man, what is good; and what doth the LORD require of thee, but to do justly, and to love mercy, and to walk humbly with thy God?

Pray about It

Temptation comes in various shapes and forms and sometimes at an unsuspecting moment. Sometimes it is sudden or it may be an ongoing battle. Thankfully, we can take such things to the Lord in prayer. There is always time for prayer. It may not be the long prayers you normally do, but a simple cry for help is all that it takes when you are pressed for time.

Joel 2:32
And it shall come to pass, that whosoever shall call on the name of the Lord shall be delivered: for in mount Zion and in Jerusalem shall be deliverance, as the Lord hath said, and in the remnant whom the Lord shall call.

Matthew 6:13
And lead us not into temptation, but deliver us from evil: For thine is the kingdom, and the power, and the glory, for ever. Amen.

Matthew 26:41
Watch and pray, that ye enter not into temptation: the spirit indeed is willing, but the flesh is weak.

Worship - Staying in His presence

Temptation happens anywhere, even in church. People lie, cheat, steal and lust anywhere. Sins that are not immediately visible can take place in the most religious of circles. However, remaining focused on God and staying in the presence of the Lord are measures which one can employ against temptation.

Psalm 16:11
Thou wilt shew me the path of life: in thy presence is fulness
of joy; at thy right hand there are pleasures for evermore.

Galatians 5:16
This I say then, Walk in the Spirit, and ye shall not fulfil the
lust of the flesh.

Ephesians 5:19
Speaking to yourselves in psalms and hymns and spiritual
songs, singing and making melody in your heart to the
Lord;

Of course, the evil one knows this, and will wait until your focus shifts. Please note, if you please, that Jesus was not tempted while He fasted, no! The evil one did not stand a chance then. Jesus was too focused. However, the evil one made an attempt to tempt Him after the fasting was over.

Matthew 4:2-3
2 And when he had fasted forty days and forty nights, he was
afterward an hungred.
3 And when the tempter came to him, he said, If thou be the
Son of God, command that these stones be made bread.

Watch therefore, be Vigilant

The evil one is persistent. His mission and mandate is to cause you to sin, and bring your soul into condemnation. We have already talked about the unclean spirit who keeps visiting his last residence (according to Matthew 12: 44) and we just read how Jesus was tempted after He fasted. Many people, even in Bible times, eventually failed, and in some instances, failure came immediately after a great victory, because they let their guard down too quickly.

One example of letting one's guard down too quickly is found in the story of Noah. Shortly after God saved Noah and his family from the flood that destroyed other living things from the face of the earth. Noah got drunk and exposed himself shamefully (Genesis 9:20 & 21).

Also, King David was enjoying some amount of peace when he too let his guard down resulting in adultery and murder (2 Samuel 11). One careless, unsuspecting moment can cost you all that you have worked so long and hard to procure.

Thomas Jefferson once said "The price of freedom is eternal vigilance."

1 Peter 5:8
Be sober, be vigilant; because your adversary the devil, as a roaring lion, walketh about, seeking whom he may devour:

Guard your Heart and Mind

You can feed your mind with the things you talk about, think about, the conversations you entertain and the things you watch. It is wise to avoid anything that the enemy can use against you. The computer programmers' rule applies here: Garbage in; garbage out.

Philippians 2:5
Let this mind be in you, which was also in Christ Jesus:

Philippians 4:8
Finally, brethren, whatsoever things are true, whatsoever things are honest, whatsoever things are just, whatsoever things are pure, whatsoever things are lovely, whatsoever things are of good report; if there be any virtue, and if there be any praise, think on these things.

The mind is a battlefield. Whether you believe it or not, there is a war going on to control your mind. Furthermore, the mind controls the behaviour.

Romans 12:2
And be not conformed to this world: but be ye transformed
by the renewing of your mind, that ye may prove what is that
good, and acceptable, and perfect, will of God.

Common Sense — Take the time to think

Then, of course, each of us should possess our fair share of
that precious commodity called common sense. The results from
the tests and temptations we receive or the experiences of our past
should remind us of our limitations. It is wise to avoid situations that
will lead to temptation. In other words, do not compromise with the
source of your temptation.

Proverbs 4:14-15
14 Enter not into the path of the wicked, and go not in the
way of evil men.
15 Avoid it, pass not by it, turn from it, and pass away.

For instance, it is foolish for one who is struggling with alcohol
to play around with liquor. Likewise, it is foolish for unmarried
saints to play around with anything that lead them into sexual sin.
Conversations, physical interactions, situations, movies, asso-
ciations that are not wholesome are seeds that, if encouraged, can
become giants in our lives should be avoided.

1 Corinthians 10:12
Wherefore let him that thinketh he standeth take heed lest he
fall.

There may be times when you have little or no control over the
situation or circumstance, but you should always have a plan in mind
that you will execute in the event your testimony for Jesus Christ is
threatened. Joseph being a slave in Egypt and a servant in Potiphar's
house could not decide when and where he would work. However,
he ran as fast as he could to avoid being seduced by his master's
wife (Genesis 39:12).

Solomon, the wisest man apart from Jesus, gave his son the following advice, with respect to temptations:

Proverbs 5:8 & 9
8 Remove thy way far from her, and come not nigh the door of her house:
9 Lest thou give thine honour unto others, and thy years unto the cruel:

Paul gave Timothy (a young man) the following advice:

2 Timothy 2:22
Flee also youthful lusts: but follow righteousness, faith, charity, peace, with them that call on the Lord out of a pure heart.

James added his voice to the warnings:

James 1:21
Wherefore lay apart all filthiness and superfluity of naughtiness, and receive with meekness the engrafted word, which is able to save your souls.

Sadly, many today are trying to see how close they can get to the edge without falling off. According to the Bible, those who are like that are simple.

Proverbs 22:3 & 27:12
A prudent man foreseeth the evil, and hideth himself: but the simple pass on, and are punished.

Help from the Holy Ghost

Sometimes God, by His Spirit, will come and rescue us from temptation. You may not always have the Word to deliver you, but God will often step in and help. Remember, He will not let the temptation get the better of you. He is 100% faithful.

Isaiah 59:19
So shall they fear the name of the Lord from the west, and his glory from the rising of the sun. When the enemy shall come in like a flood, the Spirit of the Lord shall lift up a standard against him.

Matthew 6:13
And lead us not into temptation, but deliver us from evil: For thine is the kingdom, and the power, and the glory, for ever. Amen.

Romans 8:26
Likewise the Spirit also helpeth our infirmities: for we know not what we should pray for as we ought: but the Spirit itself maketh intercession for us with groanings which cannot be uttered.

It cannot be emphasized enough that temptation will come in the form of your need. The evil one knows what you have need of and will tempt you with the opportunity to satisfy that need at the expense of offending God and jeopardizing your soul. It is simply not worth it. Resist, my brother, my sister, resist!

James 4:7
Submit yourselves therefore to God. Resist the devil, and he will flee from you.

The Benefit of being Tempted

There is an upside to temptation. This may be hard to believe knowing what the aim of temptation is. Being tempted really has its benefits, especially if we are victorious.

Romans 8:28
And we know that all things work together for good to them that love God, to them who are the called according to his purpose.

Although temptation has the capacity to bring us into sin, that is, if we yield to it; for the victorious Christians it means a building of our faith. Temptation helps to identify areas in our lives that need to be strengthened.

1 John 5:4
For whatsoever is born of God overcometh the world: and this is the victory that overcometh the world, even our faith.

Revelation 2:7, 11, & 17
7 He that hath an ear, let him hear what the Spirit saith unto the churches; To him that overcometh will I give to eat of the tree of life, which is in the midst of the paradise of God.

11 He that hath an ear, let him hear what the Spirit saith unto the churches; He that overcometh shall not be hurt of the second death.

17 He that hath an ear, let him hear what the Spirit saith unto the churches; To him that overcometh will I give to eat of the hidden manna, and will give him a white stone, and in the stone a new name written, which no man knoweth saving he that receiveth it.

CHAPTER EIGHT

THREE AREAS OF TEMPTATION

All temptations appeal to one or more of three areas of our being. These three areas are found in the following Scripture and God despises all of the things mentioned.

> *1 John 2:15 & 16*
> *15 Love not the world, neither the things that are in the world. If any man love the world, the love of the Father is not in him.*
> *16 For all that is in the world, the lust of the flesh, and the lust of the eyes, and the pride of life, is not of the Father, but is of the world.*

The evil one used all three levels of temptation: *the lust of the flesh, and the lust of the eyes, and the pride of life,* when he tempted Eve in the Garden of Eden (Genesis 3:6). He later tried them against Jesus in the wilderness (Matthew 4:1-11).

Lust of the Flesh

The lust of the flesh is the first level of battle. Many of the temptations we face in life challenge us to satisfy the needs of the flesh — our appetite or pleasure zone. If the temptation succeeds in getting your flesh involved the battle becomes more difficult. To succeed in this area you need to starve the flesh of what it seemingly needs while building up the spiritual man. Fasting helps us to focus, while abstinence builds up our self-control.

> *Genesis 25:34*
> *Then Jacob gave Esau bread and pottage of lentiles; and he did eat and drink, and rose up, and went his way: thus Esau despised his birthright.*

> *Proverbs 23:31 & 32*
> *31 Look not thou upon the wine when it is red, when it giveth his colour in the cup, when it moveth itself aright.*
> *32 At the last it biteth like a serpent, and stingeth like an adder.*

Although abstinence from food is generally what comes to mind when we speak of fasting, food can be used to represent ones appetite and the desire to satisfy the flesh. Anything that generates an ungodly inward desire should be avoided.

Lust of the Eyes

This area affects our ambitions, and if we are not careful, it will lead to covetousness. Usually, with this level of temptation, the eyes wander away from what we have towards the possessions of others. The evil one will promise wealth and fame to those who are willing to lay down their convictions for righteousness and acquire riches by dishonest means. Those who fall prey to this level of temptation are usually those who want to impress others in any way they can.

> *Genesis 39:7*
> *And it came to pass after these things, that his master's wife cast her eyes upon Joseph; and she said, Lie with me.*

Acts 8:18-20
18 And when Simon saw that through laying on of the apostles' hands the Holy Ghost was given, he offered them money,
19 Saying, Give me also this power, that on whomsoever I lay hands, he may receive the Holy Ghost.
20 But Peter said unto him, Thy money perish with thee, because thou hast thought that the gift of God may be purchased with money.

Pride of Life

This aspect, the pride of life, speaks of the ego, what one thinks of oneself, and ambition. The Scriptures have numerous warnings against pride. Right in middle of the word 'pride' is the letter 'i'.

As a small assignment, please look up the five "I's" of Lucifer found in fourteenth chapter of Isaiah, verses 13 and 14.

Proverbs 6:16-19
16 These six things doth the LORD hate: yea, seven are an abomination unto him:
17 A proud look, a lying tongue, and hands that shed innocent blood,
18 An heart that deviseth wicked imaginations, feet that be swift in running to mischief,
19 A false witness that speaketh lies, and he that soweth discord among brethren.

Proverbs 16:18
Pride goeth before destruction, and an haughty spirit before a fall.

James 4:6
But he giveth more grace. Wherefore he saith, God resisteth the proud, but giveth grace unto the humble.

Any action or desire which boosts our ego to a point where we are willing to do anything, (good or bad) to achieve it, is to be avoided. God hates any form of pride and outward show, but prefers the inner qualities, the condition of the heart and the inner man.

Psalms 51:6
Behold, thou desirest truth in the inward parts: and in the hidden part thou shalt make me to know wisdom.

Jeremiah 31:33
But this shall be the covenant that I will make with the house of Israel; After those days, saith the LORD, I will put my law in their inward parts, and write it in their hearts; and will be their God, and they shall be my people.

Promises for the Victorious Saint

It is the plan and desire of God that we all live a victorious Christian life.

The evil one has a different plan. The second and third chapters of the book of Revelation contain several promises for the victorious saint; some of which were quoted at the end of Chapter 7 of this book. But there are many more; consider the following:

Revelation 3:21
To him that overcometh will I grant to sit with me in my throne, even as I also overcame, and am set down with my Father in his throne.

2 Timothy 4:7 & 8
7 I have fought a good fight, I have finished my course, I have kept the faith:
8 Henceforth there is laid up for me a crown of righteousness, which the Lord, the righteous judge, shall give me at that day: and not to me only, but unto all them also that love his appearing.

Help for those who Fail

Of course, failure is a possibility. None of us is perfect, just forgiven. In fact, everyone one of us fail from time to time. God Almighty figured that out when He saved us. Remember, nothing takes God by surprise; He is Omniscient.

Psalm 103:14
For he knoweth our frame; he remembereth that we are dust.

Child of God, sin is all around us; but it is possible to live a sinless life. How? With Jesus' help, of course!

Hebrews 2:18
For in that he himself hath suffered being tempted, he is able to succour them that are tempted.

1 John 1:8-10
8 If we say that we have no sin, we deceive ourselves, and the truth is not in us.
9 If we confess our sins, he is faithful and just to forgive us our sins, and to cleanse us from all unrighteousness.
10 If we say that we have not sinned, we make him a liar, and his word is not in us.

1 John 2:1
My little children, these things write I unto you, that ye sin not. And if any man sin, we have an advocate with the Father, Jesus Christ the righteous:

Jude 24
Now unto him that is able to keep you from falling, and to present you faultless before the presence of his glory with exceeding joy,

The words of this old hymn, by Horatio R. Palmer, sum up this chapter on temptation.

Yield not to temptation for yielding is sin
Each victory will help you some other to win
Fight manfully onward, dark passions subdue
Look ever to Jesus He will carry you through

> Ask the Saviour to help you
> Comfort, strengthen and keep you
> He is willing to help you
> He will carry you through

Shun evil companions, bad language disdain
God's Name hold in reverence nor take it in vain
Be thoughtful and earnest, kindhearted and true
Look ever to Jesus He will carry you through

To him that o'ercometh God giveth a crown
Through faith we shall conquer though often cast down
He Who is our Saviour our strength will renew
Look ever to Jesus He will carry you through

ANOTHER QUICK ASSIGNMENT

a) Look again at the temptation of Eve and try to identify where the enemy used the lust of the flesh, the lust of the eyes and the pride of life.

Genesis 3:6
And when the woman saw that the tree was good for food, and that it was pleasant to the eyes, and a tree to be desired to make one wise, she took of the fruit thereof, and did eat, and gave also unto her husband with her; and he did eat.

b) Do the same with the passages on Jesus' temptation recorded in Matthew 4:1-11 and also in Luke 4:1-13.

c) Look at the following stories/passages in the Bible and identify the areas of temptation and whether or not the person
was victorious.

- Esau and Jacob (Genesis 25:30-34)
- Joseph & Potiphar's wife (Genesis 39:1-20)
- David and Bathsheba (2 Samuel 11:1-11)
- Ahab and Naboth (1 Kings 21:1-14)
- The rich fool (St. Luke 12:16-21)

CHAPTER NINE

THE PROBLEM OF SIN

God created Adam and Eve and placed them in the Garden of Eden in a state of complete innocence, meaning that, they had no knowledge of good or evil. They were created completely sinless yet capable of committing sin. God commanded the man not to eat *"of the tree of knowledge of good and evil"* accompanied with the warning of death should he break the command of God.

> *Genesis 2:17*
> *But of the tree of the knowledge of good and evil, thou shalt not eat of it: for in the day that thou eatest thereof thou shalt surely die.*

The evil one, Satan, tempted and deceived the woman, Eve, who then persuaded her husband, Adam, to eat of the fruit of the tree and thus they (together) broke the commandment of God (Genesis 3:1-7). This act of disobedience constitutes sin, because sin is the breaking the law of God.

> *1 John 3:4*
> *Whosoever committeth sin transgresseth also the law: for sin is the transgression of the law.*

Also, because God is righteous and his nature is holy, anything that is unrighteous and unholy is sin in the eyes of God; God hates sin.

1 John 5:17
All unrighteousness is sin: and there is a sin not unto death.

The penalty for sin is death, both spiritually and naturally. Adam died spiritually the moment he disobeyed the command of God even though he was still alive naturally. The word 'death' means 'separation', so spiritual death means that he was *spiritually* separated from God.

Isaiah 59:2
But your iniquities have separated between you and your God, and your sins have hid his face from you, that he will not hear.

Romans 6:23
For the wages of sin is death; but the gift of God is eternal life through Jesus Christ our Lord.

The Origin of Sin

There was an archangel in heaven called Lucifer and the Bible lets us know that he coveted the authority, position and power of God. Lucifer succumbed to inner temptation and led an unsuccessful revolt against God. How silly of him to even try such a thing! The Scripture points out what is called the five "I's" of Lucifer:

Isaiah 14:12-14
12 How art thou fallen from heaven, O Lucifer, son of the morning! how art thou cut down to the ground, which didst weaken the nations!
13 For thou hast said in thine heart, I will ascend into heaven, I will exalt my throne above the stars of God: I will

sit also upon the mount of the congregation, in the sides of the north:
14 I will ascend above the heights of the clouds; I will be like the most High.

There were no devils around to tempt Lucifer to do evil. Instead, iniquity developed in Lucifer, being driven by his ego and ambition. The sin of covetousness originated in him. When he lied to Eve (Genesis 3:4) he made the whole thing up himself and is therefore known as the originator or the 'father of lies'.

Ezekiel 28:14 & 15
14 Thou art the anointed cherub that covereth; and I have set thee so: thou wast upon the holy mountain of God; thou hast walked up and down in the midst of the stones of fire.
15 Thou wast perfect in thy ways from the day that thou wast created, till iniquity was found in thee.

John 8:44
Ye are of your father the devil, and the lusts of your father ye will do. He was a murderer from the beginning, and abode not in the truth, because there is no truth in him. When he speaketh a lie, he speaketh of his own: for he is a liar, and the father of it.

Fallen Angels

When God kicked Lucifer out of heaven he did not fall alone. The angels who had sided with him in his ridiculous attempt to oust God also fell.

Revelation 12:7-9
7 And there was war in heaven: Michael and his angels fought against the dragon; and the dragon fought and his angels,
8 And prevailed not; neither was their place found any more in heaven.

9 And the great dragon was cast out, that old serpent, called the Devil, and Satan, which deceiveth the whole world: he was cast out into the earth, and his angels were cast out with him.

One day while speaking with the disciples, Jesus recapped the speed with which Lucifer fell from heaven; this World record is still unbroken, a personal best for Lucifer.

Luke 10:18
And he said unto them, I beheld Satan as lightning fall from heaven.

What were they thinking? I cannot seem to get over the fact that the inner allies (pride, ego and ambition) led Lucifer to do something utterly stupid and impossible to accomplish.

How Sin entered the Human Race

Lucifer knew that God has a special love for mankind. No other creature, not even the angels in heaven, could boast of such a love. Only man can claim to be created in the likeness and image of God (see Psalm 8:4-9). Having lost his place around the throne of God for ever, Lucifer then turned his attention to man, the object of God's love, and tempted Adam and his wife, Eve, to disobey God's word. Unfortunately, Adam and Eve yielded to the temptation and that is how sin entered into the world.

Romans 5:12
Wherefore, as by one man sin entered into the world, and death by sin; and so death passed upon all men, for that all have sinned:

Adam and Eve sinned and distorted their God-given image before they became parents. As a result of the original transgression, and since then, every individual born into the world inherited this sinful nature from Adam.

Genesis 5:1- 3
1 This is the book of the generations of Adam. In the day that
God created man, in the likeness of God made he him;
2 Male and female created he them; and blessed them, and
called their name Adam, in the day when they were created.
3 And Adam lived an hundred and thirty years, and begat a
son in his own likeness, after his image; and called his name
Seth:

Romans 5:14
Nevertheless death reigned from Adam to Moses, even over
them that had not sinned after the similitude of Adam's trans-
gression, who is the figure of him that was to come.

THE CATEGORIES OF SIN

Sin is anything that is contrary to the Word of God. Sin breaks
or transgresses the Word of God and causes death, both spiritually
and physically. That's right: Sin results in death. In other words,
the existence of death is a direct result of the presence of sin in the
world.

Romans 6:23
For the wages of sin is death; but the gift of God is eternal
life through Jesus Christ our Lord.

When Adam and Eve sinned against God by transgressing
(disobeying) his Word, they died spiritually (separation from God)
before they died physically. Death, then, is simply a separation from
any source which is required to keep one functioning in a certain
realm. If we are separated from God then we are spiritually dead, for
God is a Spirit and our spiritual source.

Romans 3:23
For all have sinned, and come short of the glory of God;

If we are separated from natural life then we are physically dead. We cease to be active in the grave.

Psalm 6:5
For in death there is no remembrance of thee: in the grave who shall give thee thanks?

Sin occurs in many ways, but it falls into three main categories: inherited sin; imputed sin and committed sin. These three categories are described below.

Inherited Sin

Inherited sin means that sin is hereditary. In other words, we got it from our immediate parents, who got it from their parents, and so on, until we go right back to Adam and Eve. This is especially frightening to think that down through the years sin has been compounded and genetically downloaded from generation to generation. It implies that mankind today could be battling with issues that are foreign to him in every sense of the word.

Psalm 51:5
Behold, I was shapen in iniquity; and in sin did my mother conceive me.

Imputed Sin

Implicit in this category of sin is the idea that man is equally guilty for the sin of Adam. It suggests that we were in the loins of Adam at the time of his sin and as such we participated in the disobedience and so sin was attributed or assigned to all that were born after Adam. Notice the Scripture did not only say all are sinners, but that all have sinned.

Romans 3:23
For all have sinned, and come short of the glory of God;

For instance, think of imputed sin the same way you would think of slavery. We could not say that a slave inherited slavery from his progenitors, because slavery cannot be genetically transferred. However, every child that was born to enslaved parents was assigned the slavery treatment.

Romans 4:11
And he received the sign of circumcision, a seal of the righteousness of the faith which he had yet being uncircumcised: that he might be the father of all them that believe, though they be not circumcised; that righteousness might be imputed unto them also:

Romans 5:13
For until the law sin was in the world: but sin is not imputed when there is no law.

The subject of imputed sin is further supported in the Scriptures by the fact that Levi, one of the sons of Jacob, and grandson to Abraham, was said to have paid tithes to Melchisedec. Actually it was Abraham, his grandfather who paid the tithes, as Levi was not yet born; yet the act was *imputed* or attributed to Levi.

Hebrews 7:9 & 10
9 And as I may so say, Levi also, who receiveth tithes, payed tithes in Abraham.
10 For he was yet in the loins of his father, when Melchisedec met him.

Committed Sin

Whereas the first two categories placed and/or shared the blame for sin, this category places the problem of sin squarely at the feet of each human being. Since birth we all have contributed to the existence of sin in our world. As such we all are individually responsible for our share of sin.

Psalms 53:3
Every one of them is gone back: they are altogether become
filthy; there is none that doeth good, no, not one.

Into which category did the sin of Adam fall? Firstly, he was created sinless and was the first human being; so that took care of the matter of inherited and imputed sin. The only category of sin left for Adam and his wife is committed sin, and this happened when they yielded to the temptation of the evil one.

Other Names for Sin

Throughout the Bible you will find many other words used to denote sin. Here are a few of them but as you study your Bible you will find others.

- Evil
- Iniquity
- Wickedness
- Ungodliness
- Transgression
- Unrighteousness

CHAPTER TEN

THE WAYS AND CONSEQUENCES OF SIN

Living completely sinless is not that easy to do as long as we are in this body. The Bible states that there is nothing good in our flesh. The flesh likes to be pampered and does not like discomfort. In addition, sin takes many shapes and forms and the deception is all around. The Apostle Paul agrees, the following is what he wrote in two of his New Testament epistles:

Romans 7:19
For the good that I would I do not: but the evil which I would not, that I do.

Galatians 5:17
For the flesh lusteth against the Spirit, and the Spirit against the flesh: and these are contrary the one to the other: so that ye cannot do the things that ye would.

Sin of Omission

Friend, have you ever felt a special urge to do something that you know is right but you did not go through with it? We do not always act upon these promptings and sometimes we regret that we did not respond appropriately. Maybe it was an opportunity to witness to someone or perhaps you did not speak up for the Lord at a given time. Whatever it might have been you could have committed a sin of omission.

Luke 12:47
And that servant, which knew his lord's will, and prepared not himself, neither did according to his will, shall be beaten with many stripes.

James 4:17
Therefore to him that knoweth to do good, and doeth it not, to him it is sin.

It worth repeating: Refusal to do a right thing constitutes a sin according to the Bible.

Our Deeds are Connected to our Thoughts

I mentioned before that the mind is a battleground where wars are fought for your soul. We not only sin by committing an act, deed or speech, but also in our thoughts. Many sins originate in thoughts before they are acted out. Therefore it is important what and how we think.

Proverbs 23:7
For as he thinketh in his heart, so is he: Eat and drink, saith he to thee; but his heart is not with thee.

Proverbs 24:9
The thought of foolishness is sin: and the scorner is an abomination to men.

Romans 7:23
But I see another law in my members, warring against the law of my mind, and bringing me into captivity to the law of sin which is in my members.

However, we can still have the victory in our minds. The Scripture below shows us how:

Romans 12:2
And be not conformed to this world: but be ye transformed by the renewing of your mind, that ye may prove what is that good, and acceptable, and perfect, will of God.

The Contents of our Heart Influence our Speech

There is a correlation between our hearing and our speech. It seems what we hear enter into our hearts and what we say originate from our hearts. Isaiah attributed his unclean lips to the unclean lips of the people around him. Showing that, what those around him said, came to influence what he, in turn, said.

Isaiah 6:5
Then said I, Woe is me! for I am undone; because I am a man of unclean lips, and I dwell in the midst of a people of unclean lips: for mine eyes have seen the King, the LORD of hosts.

It is important that the heart be pure towards God and our fellow man otherwise the things we say can be sinful.

Matthew 12:34
O generation of vipers, how can ye, being evil, speak good things? for out of the abundance of the heart the mouth speaketh.

Matthew 15:19
For out of the heart proceed evil thoughts, murders, adulteries, fornications, thefts, false witness, blasphemies:

An upright heart is crucial to our victory over temptation. The Scriptures provide examples of men and women who have prayed to God for help to attain and upright heart. The Bible also offers encouragement to others to do the same.

Psalms 24:3 & 4
3 Who shall ascend into the hill of the LORD? or who shall stand in his holy place?
4 He that hath clean hands, and a pure heart; who hath not lifted up his soul unto vanity, nor sworn deceitfully.

Psalms 51:10
Create in me a clean heart, O God; and renew a right spirit within me.

Proverbs 4:23
Keep thy heart with all diligence; for out of it are the issues of life.

The conversations of Christians should be wholesome. Be very careful of the types of jokes you entertain. In our high tech society forwarding emails is a common phenomenon. Be careful not to participate into anything that will not bring glory to God.

Philippians 1:27
Only let your conversation be as it becometh the gospel of Christ: that whether I come and see you, or else be absent, I may hear of your affairs, that ye stand fast in one spirit, with one mind striving together for the faith of the gospel;

Hebrews 13:5
Let your conversation be without covetousness; and be content with such things as ye have: for he hath said, I will never leave thee, nor forsake thee.

1 Peter 2:12
Having your conversation honest among the Gentiles: that, whereas they speak against you as evildoers, they may by

*your good works, which they shall behold, glorify God in the
day of visitation.*

The Issue of Lust

From time to time we all admire someone or something, to be
honest; there is an element of desire in admiration. However, an
unhealthy preoccupation with someone or something can become
sinful. To be clear, it is sinful to envision yourself satisfying a desire
that cannot be righteously met.

Matthew 5:28
*But I say unto you, That whosoever looketh on a woman to
lust after her hath committed adultery with her already in
his heart.*

James 1:15
*Then when lust hath conceived, it bringeth forth sin: and sin,
when it is finished, bringeth forth death.*

Ignorant Sins

It is possible to sin and not even be aware of it. This is perhaps
why we are told to that each time we pray we should first forgive
others their trespasses in order to obtain forgiveness for our own.

Luke 11:4
*And forgive us our sins; for we also forgive every one that is
indebted to us. And lead us not into temptation; but deliver
us from evil.*

It is entirely possible that we have wronged someone else and
not be aware of it. However, the Holy Spirit, which is the spirit of
God, will convict us, writing His law in our hearts.

Matthew 5:23-24
23 Therefore if thou bring thy gift to the altar, and there rememberest that thy brother hath ought against thee;
24 Leave there thy gift before the altar, and go thy way; first be reconciled to thy brother, and then come and offer thy gift.

Even when we sin ignorantly, God by His spirit will bring the matter to bear on our heart so that we can repent from it.

Acts 17:30
And the times of this ignorance God winked at; but now commandeth all men every where to repent:

Philippians 3:15
Let us therefore, as many as be perfect, be thus minded: and if in any thing ye be otherwise minded, God shall reveal even this unto you.

THE EFFECTS OF SIN

Quite a lot of money, time and energy have been devoted to finding cures and solutions for certain diseases and discomforts we experience in life. There are some notorious diseases out there that will drive fear into the heart of anyone. However, the most notorious of them all is the disease called sin. All that one has to do is take a casual glimpse and it would become apparent that there are a number of things in our world today which are a direct consequence of the presence of sin. The good news is that there is a cure. Yes, the blood of Jesus and the Lord Jesus is a perfect combination against sin and its effects.

1 John 1:7
But if we walk in the light, as he is in the light, we have fellowship one with another, and the blood of Jesus Christ his Son cleanseth us from all sin.

Sin results in Confusion and Foolishness

Sin dulls the senses and causes man to forget who he is, in comparison to Almighty God. Sin resulted in Adam and Eve attempting to hide from the God, whose eyes are in every place (Proverbs 15:3). In addition, they attempted to cover themselves with leaves which would eventually fade. Sin causes man to think he is smarter than God.

Romans 2:3
And thinkest thou this, O man, that judgest them which do such things, and doest the same, that thou shalt escape the judgment of God?

1 Corinthians 3:19 & 20
19 For the wisdom of this world is foolishness with God. For it is written, He taketh the wise in their own craftiness.
20 And again, The Lord knoweth the thoughts of the wise, that they are vain.

Sin Separates Man from his God

God is too holy to dwell anywhere sin thrives. So God stays away from the man or woman who has sinned and in doing so God is also showing mercy to the sinner by sparing his life. The next time you fail to feel God's presence, the reason could be sin.

Isaiah 59:2
But your iniquities have separated between you and your God, and your sins have hid his face from you, that he will not hear.

God wants man to be like him in His holiness.

1 Peter 1:15-16
15 But as he which hath called you is holy, so be ye holy in
all manner of conversation;
16 Because it is written, Be ye holy; for I am holy.

Sin Leads to Death and Destruction

A great many lives have been ruined by sin and many have died in their sinful state and have entered a Christ-less eternity. Perversion is everywhere. Drugs, alcohol and illicit sex are main stream. Remember that sin comes with a penalty.

Ezekiel 18:20
The soul that sinneth, it shall die. The son shall not bear the iniquity of the father, neither shall the father bear the iniquity of the son: the righteousness of the righteous shall be upon him, and the wickedness of the wicked shall be upon him.

James 1:15
Then when lust hath conceived, it bringeth forth sin: and sin, when it is finished, bringeth forth death.

Sin brings Sickness

This has been a subject of much controversy. But there need not be any controversy if we carefully examine what the Scriptures have to say. Firstly, an individual's sickness may not always be a result of sin he or she has committed. Jesus clarified that with his response to the disciples concerning the man who was born blind, and so did Job to his friends.

John 9:1-3
1 And as Jesus passed by, he saw a man which was blind from his birth.

2 And his disciples asked him, saying, Master, who did sin, this man, or his parents, that he was born blind?
3 Jesus answered, Neither hath this man sinned, nor his parents: but that the works of God should be made manifest in him.

However, the presence of sickness in the world, in general, is a direct result of sin. At times, an individual's sickness can be traced to a current or past lifestyle. This is what Jesus said to the man who had been sick for thirty eight (38) years:

John 5:14
Afterward Jesus findeth him in the temple, and said unto him, Behold, thou art made whole: sin no more, lest a worse thing come unto thee.

James, the brother of our Lord, weighed in on the subject of sin and had this to say:

James 5:15
And the prayer of faith shall save the sick, and the Lord shall raise him up; and if he have committed sins, they shall be forgiven him.

CHAPTER ELEVEN

DEALING WITH SIN

Now that we know what sin is, the many ways we sin and what sin will do to us, the next step is to explore how to get rid of the sin we have committed, inherited and imputed unto us. Sin is a deadly 'disease'; if untreated, it can damage many areas of our lives and eventually us. The Bible has some instructions that we can use to effectively remove sin, its stain and guilt, from our lives.

Confession is Good for the Soul

The Christian pathway is a journey, some days you might be on the mountain and on other days you might be in the valley. God knows that we will not always be the strong and victorious children of God that we can be everyday. However, if and when we sin against God we should always confess our sin to Him and receive forgiveness so we can proceed with our Christian lives.

1 John 1:9
If we confess our sins, he is faithful and just to forgive us our sins, and to cleanse us from all unrighteousness.

1 John 2:1
My little children, these things write I unto you, that ye sin not. And if any man sin, we have an advocate with the Father, Jesus Christ the righteous:

Admit it, Quit it, and Forget it

Acknowledging and confessing ones transgression are the first two steps in the redemption process, but they are not sufficient; there is a yet another step to take. Forsaking the sin and turning away from any semblance of it is necessary to break the hold of that particular sin off the believer's life. Those who are serious about redemption will accept God's help to gain the victory over their past sins.

Psalms 103:12 & 13
12 As far as the east is from the west, so far hath he removed our transgressions from us.
13 Like as a father pitieth his children, so the LORD pitieth them that fear him.

Proverbs 28:13
He that covereth his sins shall not prosper: but whoso confesseth and forsaketh them shall have mercy.

Luke 17:3
Take heed to yourselves: If thy brother trespass against thee, rebuke him; and if he repent, forgive him.

Forgiveness Received is directly linked to Forgiveness Granted

Jesus gives an example about forgiveness in His dealings with the Apostle Peter. Peter was the disciple who denied knowing the Lord Jesus. He was one of the few who were on the inner circle; he even walked on water. Yet he denied knowing the Lord, not once, not twice, but three times. Jesus had prophesied that this would happen.

Luke 22:61 & 62
61 And the Lord turned, and looked upon Peter. And Peter remembered the word of the Lord, how he had said unto him, Before the cock crow, thou shalt deny me thrice.
62 And Peter went out, and wept bitterly.

After the resurrection, prior to being caught up into heaven, Jesus encountered Peter again and forgave him for the denial. We too are able to praise the Lord today because God also forgave our sins. In turn, we ought to forgive others who have wronged us. In fact, in order for us to be truly forgiven, we must forgive those who have trespassed against us.

Matthew 6:15
But if ye forgive not men their trespasses, neither will your Father forgive your trespasses.

Jesus taught another beautiful lesson on forgiveness found in Matthew 18:21-35. After reading this gripping tale, you will understand why it is so important not to hold grudges.

Confide in a Good Source

If you need spiritual counsel and guidance, speak to your pastor, someone your pastor recommends or someone you can trust and who will be able to help you grow. This is particularly important because certain personal information in the hands of the wrong people can be used to create havoc and damage a person's character and image, and may even ruin his or her life.

James 5:16
Confess your faults one to another, and pray one for another, that ye may be healed. The effectual fervent prayer of a righteous man availeth much.

This is why you need to be covered in prayer. It is imperative that your local church has suitably qualified people on staff who have been recognized by the church as trained counselors who can provide the right mix of counsel and encouragement for those who are trying to deal with a specific sin.

Restoration

Jesus not only forgave Peter but also restored him. Forgiving someone is not enough. Many of us may have forgiven someone who has wronged us but the manner in which we behave towards that individual will show whether or not we have truly and fully forgiven him or her.

Restoring something means bringing it back to its original form; and so it is with the individual transgressor. Restoring transgressors means that we no longer see them in the wrong and we do not keep reminding them of the wrong they have done. Here is how the Master Forgiver handled the disciple who denied knowing Him.

> *John 21:15-17*
> *15 So when they had dined, Jesus saith to Simon Peter, Simon, son of Jonas, lovest thou me more than these? He saith unto him, Yea, Lord; thou knowest that I love thee. He saith unto him, Feed my lambs.*
> *16 He saith to him again the second time, Simon, son of Jonas, lovest thou me? He saith unto him, Yea, Lord; thou knowest that I love thee. He saith unto him, Feed my sheep.*
> *17 He saith unto him the third time, Simon, son of Jonas, lovest thou me? Peter was grieved because he said unto him the third time, Lovest thou me? And he said unto him, Lord, thou knowest all things; thou knowest that I love thee. Jesus saith unto him, Feed my sheep.*

The other disciples also accepted Jesus' decision regarding Peter and embraced him as fellow apostle as if nothing happened. In fact, that is exactly what it means to be justified. Through the blood of Jesus, God sees me *"just-as-if-I'd"* (justified) never sinned. After restoring the Apostle Peter, do you read anywhere in the Scriptures where his denial of Jesus was brought up again? The other disciples supported his preaching on the day of Pentecost.

> *Acts 2:14*
> *But Peter, standing up with the eleven, lifted up his voice, and said unto them, Ye men of Judaea, and all ye that dwell at Jerusalem, be this known unto you, and hearken to my words:*

DEALING WITH THE GUILT OF THE PAST

Receiving God's forgiveness is more than just a good feeling. The truth is that sometimes you may not feel like you have been forgiven. And guess what, the evil one will use that feeling to weigh you down. Yet, if we confess our sins to God the Bible states that He will forgive us. And that's more than feelings; that is a fact. God is faithful to His word, make that 100% faithful.

> *1 John 1:9*
> *If we confess our sins, he is faithful and just to forgive us our sins, and to cleanse us from all unrighteousness.*

> *1 John 3:20*
> *For if our heart condemn us, God is greater than our heart, and knoweth all things.*

My Conscience is Alive

Having a live conscience is a good thing. It is a sign that the Holy Spirit is still at work in your life. God also works with the conscience to bring conviction into ones life about specific things. Those who have constantly ignored that conviction have weakened their conscience by their deeds.

1 Timothy 4:1-2
1 Now the Spirit speaketh expressly, that in the latter times some shall depart from the faith, giving heed to seducing spirits, and doctrines of devils;
2 Speaking lies in hypocrisy; having their conscience seared with a hot iron;

The guilt of sin sometimes causes us to feel unworthy and that should be a natural feeling or reaction. The day you do something that you discovered was an offense to God and a violation of His word, and do not feel any kind of remorse, you should be concerned. That means you no longer care about the things of God and your heart has become hard.

Proverbs 29:1
He, that being often reproved hardeneth his neck, shall suddenly be destroyed, and that without remedy.

Romans 1:28
And even as they did not like to retain God in their knowledge, God gave them over to a reprobate mind, to do those things which are not convenient;

Likely to re-Offend

There are some sins which may have very deep roots into the life of some individuals such as an addiction to something evil; these are not easily broken. These are like strongholds which the individual must consciously battle with a steady, deliberate regiment of prayer and fasting. Coupled with the Word of God, a sound support system and a strong determination to overcome, victory can be won.

Mark 9:28-29
28 And when he was come into the house, his disciples asked him privately, Why could not we cast him out?
29 And he said unto them, This kind can come forth by nothing, but by prayer and fasting.

Jude 1:24
Now unto him that is able to keep you from falling, and to present you faultless before the presence of his glory with exceeding joy,

Remember, you do not have to fail. The evil one will keep trying. He knows you have been weak before; but so do you. Since you know what your area of weakness is, it would be wise for you to put some safeguards in place to help you overcome each temptation. Be conscious and decisive. God is able to keep you. Trust Him totally today!

O Love of God

Being overly remorseful can sometimes result in depression. There are people who the evil one has convinced that they are beyond the scope of God's love. Yes, he comes along and makes you feel like God does not love you. But friend, that is a lie. God loved you before you knew anything about His righteousness. He knows all there is to know about you (past, present and future), and He loved you anyway.

Romans 5:8
But God commendeth his love toward us, in that, while we were yet sinners, Christ died for us.

1 John 4:19
We love him, because he first loved us.

If you are a parent you will understand the disappointment that comes along when you child does something really wrong. But do you hate or cast off your child because of that? No, you do not. Sometimes you employ the tough love approach and let the child suffer a little. The loving parent will always find a way to restore the fellowship.

Isaiah 49:15
Can a woman forget her sucking child, that she should not have compassion on the son of her womb? yea, they may forget, yet will I not forget thee.

Lamentations 3:31 & 32
31 For the Lord will not cast off for ever:
32 But though he cause grief, yet will he have compassion according to the multitude of his mercies.

Thankfully, our God is a loving God. He epitomizes love. He is love Himself. If it was not for the love of God none of us would be able to stand today, because as much as we try, at one point or another we have failed God, yet He still loves us.

Romans 8:35-39
35 Who shall separate us from the love of Christ? shall tribulation, or distress, or persecution, or famine, or nakedness, or peril, or sword?
36 As it is written, For thy sake we are killed all the day long; we are accounted as sheep for the slaughter.
37 Nay, in all these things we are more than conquerors through him that loved us.
38 For I am persuaded, that neither death, nor life, nor angels, nor principalities, nor powers, nor things present, nor things to come,
39 Nor height, nor depth, nor any other creature, shall be able to separate us from the love of God, which is in Christ Jesus our Lord.

Do not be Presumptuous

There are some, however, who only teach the love of God. They fail to advise their audience that God is also to be feared.

Deuteronomy 4:24
For the LORD thy God is a consuming fire, even a jealous God.

Deuteronomy 10:17
For the LORD your God is God of gods, and Lord of lords, a great God, a mighty, and a terrible, which regardeth not persons, nor taketh reward:

We should never sin presumptuously believing that we can simply go to God and ask for forgiveness. Some people do that; but deliberate sin is dangerous thing. David prayed that God would keep him back from such a sin while the Apostle Peter spoke more about it.

Psalm 19:13
Keep back thy servant also from presumptuous sins; let them not have dominion over me: then shall I be upright, and I shall be innocent from the great transgression.

2 Peter 2:10
But chiefly them that walk after the flesh in the lust of uncleanness, and despise government. Presumptuous are they, self-willed, they are not afraid to speak evil of dignities.

Living in a period of grace is no excuse to continue in sin. God is merciful and longsuffering as we already discovered, but we should ensure that we "...*do not frustrate the grace of God...*" Galatians 2:21a.

Romans 6:1-2
1 What shall we say then? Shall we continue in sin, that grace may abound?
2 God forbid. How shall we, that are dead to sin, live any longer therein?

Sin is not a game; it is deadly. We learned in the previous section that sin that is constantly and deliberately repeated and not repented of can lead to hardened hearts and reprobate minds. There comes a time when we will have to grow up and face the consequences of our sin and understand that there is no guarantee that when we 'get ready' to repent that we will find repentance.

Hebrews 12:16-17
16 Lest there be any fornicator, or profane person, as Esau, who for one morsel of meat sold his birthright.
17 For ye know how that afterward, when he would have inherited the blessing, he was rejected: for he found no place of repentance, though he sought it carefully with tears.

ANOTHER QUICK ASSIGNMENT

It is impossible to name all the sins in the world today but I have listed a few of them below. As an exercise you could try to find examples of these in the Bible for yourself and write the Scripture references beside each one.

Apostasy _____
Blasphemy_____
Covetousness_____
Deception _____
Envy _____
Fornication _____
Hatred _____
Jealousy_____
Lust _____
Murder_____

With the help your Bible teacher and a dictionary try to determine the meaning of the words above and ways to avoid committing them.

CHAPTER TWELVE

THE JUDGMENT OF GOD

Now, as much as God is a loving God, He will not tolerate sin. The evil one has successfully deceived many today into thinking that a loving God will not punish them for the evils they continue to do. God is also a God of Judgment. He is the Righteous Judge.

2 Timothy 4:8
Henceforth there is laid up for me a crown of righteousness, which the Lord, the righteous judge, shall give me at that day: and not to me only, but unto all them also that love his appearing.

As it was in the Days of Noah

The Scriptures declare that as a result of sin God destroyed the Earth. This happened in the days of Noah (Genesis 6-9).

Genesis 6:5 & 6
5 And God saw that the wickedness of man was great in the earth, and that every imagination of the thoughts of his heart was only evil continually.
6 And it repented the Lord that he had made man on the earth, and it grieved him at his heart.

God destroyed the whole earth with a flood but promised that He would not use a flood to destroy the earth again. Only Noah, his family and the animals that were in the ark, were saved; and as a token of His promise, God created the rainbow.

Genesis 9:13-15
13 I do set my bow in the cloud, and it shall be for a token of a covenant between me and the earth.
14 And it shall come to pass, when I bring a cloud over the earth, that the bow shall be seen in the cloud:
15 And I will remember my covenant, which is between me and you and every living creature of all flesh; and the waters shall no more become a flood to destroy all flesh.

The activities of Noah's day are happening again just as Jesus prophesied.

Matthew 24:37-39
37 But as the days of Noe were, so shall also the coming of the Son of man be.
38 For as in the days that were before the flood they were eating and drinking, marrying and giving in marriage, until the day that Noe entered into the ark,
39 And knew not until the flood came, and took them all away; so shall also the coming of the Son of man be.

Many more things are happening in the world today. Kindly read Romans 1:16-32. See if you can identify, from the things mentioned, anything that is still happening today. You will find, among other things,

- Idolatry (Romans 1:25)
- Homosexuality (Romans 1:26 & 27)

The list above is by no means exhaustive (see also 1 Corinthians 6: 9 & 10 and Galatians 5: 19-21). Yet those sins and others have corrupted the Earth and God intends to destroy it.

So shall it be in the End

The Earth is destined for destruction. Leaders of powerful nations around the world are positioning themselves against each other. The threat of nuclear war is fast becoming less of a threat and more of a reality with every passing day. Our natural resources are being depleted to make room for mega cities, mega churches, mega malls and coliseums. Animals are losing their natural habitats. Wildlife is threatened by extinction, while the environment has become a hot button election issue.

There is an increase in the types, frequency and intensity of what are commonly called, 'acts of God' – forest fires, tornados, hurricanes, tsunamis, typhoons, earthquakes and so on. Plus, there is a new kid on the block called, Global Warming, which is now featured prominently on the major news channels. The icy regions are melting and the run offs have increased shore lines around the world. Low lying areas are in danger of being covered up by the oceans' waves.

To say nothing of the seemingly increasing list of diseases which threaten our very existence and rob us, from time to time, of our loved ones. Death almost appears to be laughing in the face of our medical advancements as we stand helpless, having no response to what is going on. The Earth is getting ready for something big. Too many things are happening all at once. Almost as if there is a rush to meet a deadline.

The world is in a crisis. War, strife, murder, incidents and accidents, are now common place. The financial markets are going through turbulence and the future for many is uncertain. Many people who were getting ready to retire are working longer while others are rejoining the workforce.

Matthew 24:6-8
6 And ye shall hear of wars and rumours of wars: see that ye be not troubled: for all these things must come to pass, but the end is not yet.

7 For nation shall rise against nation, and kingdom against kingdom: and there shall be famines, and pestilences, and earthquakes, in divers places.
8 All these are the beginning of sorrows.

In addition to all these natural disasters just named, God shall also purge this Earth with fire.

2 Peter 3:10
But the day of the Lord will come as a thief in the night; in the which the heavens shall pass away with a great noise, and the elements shall melt with fervent heat, the earth also and the works that are therein shall be burned up.

Revelation 21:1
And I saw a new heaven and a new earth: for the first heaven and the first earth were passed away; and there was no more sea.

Before the Destruction

The Bible teaches that God will have a harvest and He will keep the good and destroy the evil. It will be cleaning up time; similar to what we do when it is time for a renovation. We go through the pile of stuff we have and separate the things we plan to keep from those we intend to discard.

Matthew 13:41-43
41 The Son of man shall send forth his angels, and they shall gather out of his kingdom all things that offend, and them which do iniquity;
42 And shall cast them into a furnace of fire: there shall be wailing and gnashing of teeth.
43 Then shall the righteous shine forth as the sun in the kingdom of their Father. Who hath ears to hear, let him hear.

So, before the renovation of the Earth begins, God will do a separation; the sheep from the goats; the wheat from the tares; the saints from the sinners. He will save the saints and punish the ungodly. For how long? Forever and ever and ever.

Matthew 25:32-34 & 41
32 And before him shall be gathered all nations: and he shall separate them one from another, as a shepherd divideth his sheep from the goats:
33 And he shall set the sheep on his right hand, but the goats on the left.
34 Then shall the King say unto them on his right hand, Come, ye blessed of my Father, inherit the kingdom prepared for you from the foundation of the world:

41 Then shall he say also unto them on the left hand, Depart from me, ye cursed, into everlasting fire, prepared for the devil and his angels:

CHAPTER THIRTEEN

A PLACE CALLED HELL

God prepared a place called 'hell' for the devil and his angels (Matthew 25:41). Hell is definitely not a nice place. Friend, you do not want to go to hell; nobody does. It is a place of no return, nobody gets out of hell. It's one way and it is a dead end. The Bible says hell has fervent fire, worms, torments, unquenchable thirst and unanswered prayers.

Mark 9:43 & 44
43 And if thy hand offend thee, cut it off: it is better for thee to enter into life maimed, than having two hands to go into hell, into the fire that never shall be quenched:
44 Where their worm dieth not, and the fire is not quenched.

Luke 16:23-26
23 And in hell he lift up his eyes, being in torments, and seeth Abraham afar off, and Lazarus in his bosom.
24 And he cried and said, Father Abraham, have mercy on me, and send Lazarus, that he may dip the tip of his finger in water, and cool my tongue; for I am tormented in this flame.
25 But Abraham said, Son, remember that thou in thy life-time receivedst thy good things, and likewise Lazarus evil things: but now he is comforted, and thou art tormented.

26 And beside all this, between us and you there is a great gulf fixed: so that they which would pass from hence to you cannot; neither can they pass to us, that would come from thence.

Residents of Hell

We know that hell was not initially prepared for man. Man was created to spend time with God. Hell was prepared for the devil (the evil one) and his (fallen) angels (Matthew 25:41). These angelic beings were not spared the wrath and judgment of God.

2 Peter 2:4
For if God spared not the angels that sinned, but cast them down to hell, and delivered them into chains of darkness, to be reserved unto judgment;

Jude 1:6
And the angels which kept not their first estate, but left their own habitation, he hath reserved in everlasting chains under darkness unto the judgment of the great day.

Those people who choose to follow the evil one and rebel against God will join that devil in hell. By their deeds they have made reservations for hell.

Psalm 9:17
The wicked shall be turned into hell, and all the nations that forget God.

Choose Life

Humans were actually born to die. We were born in sin; and the penalty for sin is death. So, from birth to death, one does not have to do anything to be condemned. However, in order to live, we must choose life. There is no automatic plan for salvation.

Deuteronomy 30:19
I call heaven and earth to record this day against you, that
I have set before you life and death, blessing and cursing:
therefore choose life, that both thou and thy seed may live

Joshua 24:15
And if it seem evil unto you to serve the LORD, choose you
this day whom ye will serve; whether the gods which your
fathers served that were on the other side of the flood, or the
gods of the Amorites, in whose land ye dwell: but as for me
and my house, we will serve the LORD.

1 Kings 18:21
And Elijah came unto all the people, and said, How long halt
ye between two opinions? if the LORD be God, follow him:
but if Baal, then follow him. And the people answered him
not a word.

Hell is Booming

Sin can be sweet. We might as well admit it. But the cost of sin can be as much as our lives and last for eternity. So many people today are still living it up in sin and pleasure. There is no shortage of entertainment on the planet. Sadly, so many people are on their way to hell and may not even know it.

Matthew 7:13
Enter ye in at the strait gate: for wide is the gate, and broad
is the way, that leadeth to destruction, and many there be
which go in thereat:

As a result of the increasing numbers going through that wide gate leading down that 'broad way', hell, is constantly under renovation, expanding to make room for new arrivals.

Proverbs 27:20
Hell and destruction are never full; so the eyes of man are never satisfied.

Isaiah 5:14
Therefore hell hath enlarged herself, and opened her mouth without measure: and their glory, and their multitude, and their pomp, and he that rejoiceth, shall descend into it.

Isaiah 14:9
Hell from beneath is moved for thee to meet thee at thy coming: it stirreth up the dead for thee, even all the chief ones of the earth; it hath raised up from their thrones all the kings of the nations.

Hell and the Grave

There are certain words that were translated as *hell* in the Authorized Version of the Bible that, in fact, refer to the 'grave'. But there really is a red, hot hell that burns for all eternity. Hell is different from the grave; they are not one and the same. With the help of a few Scriptures let us underscore the main differences between hell and the grave.

1. Firstly, only the dead body goes into a grave, but the soul can be cast into hell.

Matthew 10:28
And fear not them which kill the body, but are not able to kill the soul: but rather fear him which is able to destroy both soul and body in hell.

Luke 12:4 & 5
4 And I say unto you my friends, Be not afraid of them that kill the body, and after that have no more that they can do.

5 But I will forewarn you whom ye shall fear: Fear him, which after he hath killed hath power to cast into hell; yea, I say unto you, Fear him.

2. Secondly, residents of hell will be conscious, while those in the grave are dead.

Psalm 115:17
The dead praise not the Lord, neither any that go down into silence.

Luke 16:23
And in hell he lift up his eyes, being in torments, and seeth Abraham afar off, and Lazarus in his bosom.

3. Thirdly, there is no feeling in the grave, but torments exist in hell.

Ecclesiastes 9:10
Whatsoever thy hand findeth to do, do it with thy might; for there is no work, nor device, nor knowledge, nor wisdom, in the grave, whither thou goest.

Luke 16:24
And he cried and said, Father Abraham, have mercy on me, and send Lazarus, that he may dip the tip of his finger in water, and cool my tongue; for I am tormented in this flame.

4. Fourthly, amnesia will be in the grave, but memory will also be a source of torment in hell.

Psalm 6:5
For in death there is no remembrance of thee: in the grave who shall give thee thanks?

Luke 16:25
But Abraham said, Son, remember that thou in thy lifetime
receivedst thy good things, and likewise Lazarus evil things:
but now he is comforted, and thou art tormented.

5. Finally, a body can be exhumed from the grave, but hell has
    no escape routes.

Matthew 28:13
Saying, Say ye, His disciples came by night, and stole him
away while we slept.

That was the script the chief priests and elders of the people
gave to the soldiers who guarded the tomb of Jesus.

John 12:17
The people therefore that was with him when he called
Lazarus out of his grave, and raised him from the dead, bare
record.

Luke 16:26
And beside all this, between us and you there is a great
gulf fixed: so that they which would pass from hence to you
cannot; neither can they pass to us, that would come from
thence.

ANOTHER QUICK ASSIGNMENT

As you read you own Bible, see what other differences there are
between hell and the grave. Make a list of these differences and their
Scripture references.

CHAPTER FOURTEEN

HEAVEN BELONGS TO YOU

Okay, so we know that the Earth will be entirely renovated. The first time God did some renovation (Noah's day) He washed evil men off the face of the earth with a flood. Only Noah and his family were saved; every other creature upon the face of the earth drowned.

Genesis 7:23
And every living substance was destroyed which was upon the face of the ground, both man, and cattle, and the creeping things, and the fowl of the heaven; and they were destroyed from the earth: and Noah only remained alive, and they that were with him in the ark.

He also destroyed Sodom and Gomorrah; these cities and their inhabitants perished in the flames.

Genesis 19:24 & 25
24 Then the LORD rained upon Sodom and upon Gomorrah brimstone and fire from the LORD out of heaven;
25 And he overthrew those cities, and all the plain, and all the inhabitants of the cities, and that which grew upon the ground.

Similarly, when God gets ready to destroy this earth, He will take the church (the saints) out but the sinners and the ungodly shall be burned up. Dear reader, this is why we preach, teach and witness to people and warn them of the coming judgment.

2 Corinthians 5:11
Knowing therefore the terror of the Lord, we persuade men; but we are made manifest unto God; and I trust also are made manifest in your consciences.

God did not create man to destroy him. Not at all! Man was created to love the Lord with all his heart, soul and might. God does not want man to perish that is why Jesus came into the world. You see, man lost the first round to the evil one in the Garden of Eden, but Jesus came and won back that which was lost.

Titus 2:13-14
13 Looking for that blessed hope, and the glorious appearing of the great God and our Saviour Jesus Christ;
14 Who gave himself for us, that he might redeem us from all iniquity, and purify unto himself a peculiar people, zealous of good works.

2 Peter 3:9
The Lord is not slack concerning his promise, as some men count slackness; but is longsuffering to us-ward, not willing that any should perish, but that all should come to repentance.

Heaven is such a Wonderful Place

Heaven is where the saints will be while God renovates the earth. Heaven is where God reigns.

Psalm 11:4
The Lord is in his holy temple, the Lord's throne is in heaven: his eyes behold, his eyelids try, the children of men.

Acts 7:49
Heaven is my throne, and earth is my footstool: what house
will ye build me? saith the Lord: or what is the place of my
rest?

Heaven is such a beautiful place. It is the place I want to be.
There will be no sorrow in heaven. There will be no hunger; no lack.
Hallelujah!

Revelation 7:16 & 17
16 They shall hunger no more, neither thirst any more;
neither shall the sun light on them, nor any heat.
17 For the Lamb which is in the midst of the throne shall feed
them, and shall lead them unto living fountains of waters:
and God shall wipe away all tears from their eyes.

The New Jerusalem

The Bible states that God will prepare a new heaven and a new
earth.

Revelation 21:1
And I saw a new heaven and a new earth: for the first heaven
and the first earth were passed away; and there was no more
sea.

Then out of the new heaven God will present upon the new earth
a new city called the New Jerusalem.

What is this City like?

Revelation chapter 21 tells us about this city. I am not just content
to sing or read about it. I really want to go there. I am in no hurry,
but when the Lord is ready I want to experience what this bright
celestial city is like.

- God will tabernacle with His people (vs. 3)
- There will be no sorrow there (vs. 4)
- It will be very bright with the glory of God (vs. 11)
- The City will be squared with a great high wall with twelve foundations each bearing the name of one of the Apostles (vs. 12, 14, 16 & 18-20)
- There will be three pearly gates on each side and each gate is manned by an angel named after a tribe in Israel (vs. 12, 13 & 21)
- The streets of the city will be made of gold (vs. 21)
- The Lamb will be the Temple (vs. 22)
- No sunlight will be needed because God is the light (vs. 23)
- Only the saints can enter (vs. 27)

The description continues in chapter 22.

- There will be a river of life flowing out of God's throne (vs. 1 & 2)
- There will be the tree of life on either side of river, which bears twelve kinds of fruits and the leaves are for the healing of the nations (vs. 2 & 3)
- There will be no night there (vs. 5)

CHAPTER FIFTEEN

GOD'S SALVATION PLAN

What does it mean to be saved? Saved from what? These are but a few of the questions that are often asked whenever the subject of salvation comes up. So let us answer these questions so we can prayerfully put God's plan for salvation into action.

A Brief Recap

We already mentioned that mankind is God's prized possession. God loves mankind but He hates sin. We also saw how sin entered into the world when our first parents yielded to temptation and ate the forbidden fruit. Finally, we know that the holiness of God will not allow sin to dominate the earth forever and that God will destroy the earth, turn the sinners into hell with the devil and his angels, and relocate the righteous to the place He went to prepare for them.

John 14:2 & 3
2 In my Father's house are many mansions: if it were not so,
I would have told you. I go to prepare a place for you.
3 And if I go and prepare a place for you, I will come again,
and receive you unto myself; that where I am, there ye may
be also.

Not One Righteous

Every human being born after Adam and Eve were born as sinners. We inherited the sinful nature from our progenitors. We have all sinned.

Romans 3:10
As it is written, There is none righteous, no, not one:

Galatians 3:22
But the scripture hath concluded all under sin, that the promise by faith of Jesus Christ might be given to them that believe.

Even the tiny little baby just coming into the world has a sinful nature and is prone to do evil things. It is much like buying a potted plant at the local garden store and taking it home. Before long you will notice that there are other things coming up out of the soil that you did not know were there. As it is with soil, so it is with this flesh; maybe because man is made from the dust of the earth (soil). There is nothing good in our flesh.

Romans 7:18
For I know that in me (that is, in my flesh,) dwelleth no good thing: for to will is present with me; but how to perform that which is good I find not.

The flesh will surprise you. Someone should have warned Esau that the flesh would cause him to give up his birthright for a 'mess of pottage' (Genesis 25: 29 - 34).

David, too, allowed the flesh to get the better of him to the point that he committed adultery and plotted the murder of the woman's husband when he discovered that he got her pregnant (2 Samuels 11). Wow, is that really in the Bible?, you may ask. It sure is! But that is how dangerous this flesh can become! Here's how to handle the flesh:

Romans 6:12
Let not sin therefore reign in your mortal body, that ye should obey it in the lusts thereof.

Romans 13:14
But put ye on the Lord Jesus Christ, and make not provision for the flesh, to fulfil the lusts thereof.

The Apostle Paul shared the following self-imposed discipline tool with the Corinthian church; I would like to appreciate the apostle for being so overtly honest. We have too many saints pretending to be Superman and Wonder Woman. Superman had to deal with kryptonite, so each of us must deal with whatever challenges we face.

1 Corinthians 9:27
But I keep under my body, and bring it into subjection: lest that by any means, when I have preached to others, I myself should be a castaway.

God's First Major Challenge

The presence of sin in our lives separates us from God and sets us apart and in line for His wrath and judgment. This is exactly the kind of situation that the evil one simply loves to exploit. Satan lost his place in heaven because of sin and can never regain it. Instead he has a permanent reservation in hell. He who was once called the 'son of the morning' and enjoyed worshipping around the throne of God while basking in His manifested presence, is now a ruler of darkness and has been relegated to the lowly pits of hell where the fire, and even the worms, never die. What a loss!

Isaiah 14:12
How art thou fallen from heaven, O Lucifer, son of the morning! how art thou cut down to the ground, which didst weaken the nations!

Ephesians 6:12
For we wrestle not against flesh and blood, but against prin-
cipalities, against powers, against the rulers of the darkness
of this world, against spiritual wickedness in high places.

Since the evil one cannot hurt God he has directed his efforts towards hurting what God loves. Satan knows that God hates sin but loves the man He created. If the evil one could get what God hates (sin) into what God loves (man) then God might have a problem dealing with that.

So, he tempted man and was successful in getting him to sin. Remember, sin results in death, so when man sinned, the justice of God demanded that man should die. Actually, that situation put God in a dilemma: He hates sin but loves man. But the man He loves has sin in his life. If He spares man, sin will flourish. If He kills man He will get rid of sin but will also lose the man He loves. What should God do?

I Need a Substitute

God had to find a way to accomplish two things; that is, saving man, yet pacifying His wrath on sin.

Genesis 3:21
Unto Adam also and to his wife did the Lord God make coats
of skins, and clothed them.

God placed the penalty of sin (which is death) upon an inno-cent animal, and thereby man escaped the punishment for his own sin. This is what is known in theological circles as the 'Law of Substitution'. An innocent animal died for the sin it did not commit, while Adam received pardon for the sin he did commit and God was pacified in knowing that sin did not go unpunished but His man was spared. What a mighty God we serve!

Galatians 2:20
I am crucified with Christ: nevertheless I live; yet not I, but
Christ liveth in me: and the life which I now live in the flesh
I live by the faith of the Son of God, who loved me, and gave
himself for me.

In the chapter on sin, we mentioned that Adam and Eve used leaves to cover their nakedness and attempted to hide from the Omnipresent God. To say nothing of such fallacy, their action also underscores the intelligence of man in attempting to find a solution for himself; yet foolish enough to think he could hide from God. Sin really does dull the senses.

Romans 1:22
Professing themselves to be wise, they became fools,

The significance of Genesis 3:21 quoted above however, is to point out that an animal died in order that skins could be provided. The substitute animal certainly was not deserving of death, the wages of sin (Romans 6:23), because it did no wrong. In essence, God switched the guilt and the death that Adam and Eve deserved, with the innocence and life that that creature enjoyed, and in doing so He saved the man and still pacified His wrath by fulfilling the penalty of sin.

WHAT MUST I DO TO BE SAVED?

Using the Adam and Eve story as an example, you will notice how God kept talking to man until he acknowledged his sin and explained why he was trying to hide from God. Today, God is still speaking; He is speaking through the Word of God and even nature itself. Really, mankind has no excuse. We have more preachers today than we had before. The gospel is in print; it's on the big screen; it's everywhere; so there is really no excuse.

Luke 16:27 - 31
27 Then he said, I pray thee therefore, father, that thou wouldest send him to my father's house:
28 For I have five brethren; that he may testify unto them, lest they also come into this place of torment.
29 Abraham saith unto him, They have Moses and the prophets; let them hear them.
30 And he said, Nay, father Abraham: but if one went unto them from the dead, they will repent.
31 And he said unto him, If they hear not Moses and the prophets, neither will they be persuaded, though one rose from the dead.

Romans 1:20
For the invisible things of him from the creation of the world are clearly seen, being understood by the things that are made, even his eternal power and Godhead; so that they are without excuse:

Hebrews 1:1 & 2
1 God, who at sundry times and in divers manners spake in time past unto the fathers by the prophets,
2 Hath in these last days spoken unto us by his Son, whom he hath appointed heir of all things, by whom also he made the worlds;

Acknowledge the Sin

The first step toward salvation is for one to acknowledge or admit that he or she is guilty and deserving of the destruction mentioned in the Word of God. In the same token one must recognize that he or she is in need of a Saviour. Thank God, there is a Saviour in Jesus Christ.

Genesis 3:9 & 10
9 And the LORD God called unto Adam, and said unto him, Where art thou?

10 And he said, I heard thy voice in the garden, and I was afraid, because I was naked; and I hid myself.

Psalm 51:3
For I acknowledge my transgressions: and my sin is ever before me.

Recognize God's Mercy

It is also important to acknowledge and recognize that the reason we have not yet been punished or destroyed is not because we have not sinned, or that God did not see our sin, but it is solely because of the grace, mercy and longsuffering of God.

Psalm 103:10
He hath not dealt with us after our sins; nor rewarded us according to our iniquities.

Ecclesiastes 8:11
Because sentence against an evil work is not executed speedily, therefore the heart of the sons of men is fully set in them to do evil.

Lamentations 3:22 & 23
22 It is of the Lord's mercies that we are not consumed, because his compassions fail not.
23 They are new every morning: great is thy faithfulness.

2 Peter 3:9
The Lord is not slack concerning his promise, as some men count slackness; but is longsuffering to us-ward, not willing that any should perish, but that all should come to repentance.

Revelations 2:21
And I gave her space to repent of her fornication; and she repented not.

God in His mercy knows also that some people do not know the Word of God, and that is perhaps why He has spared some of us despite the evil of our ways. The Apostle Paul admitted that he did some things in ignorance:

1 Timothy 1:13
Who was before a blasphemer, and a persecutor, and injurious: but I obtained mercy, because I did it ignorantly in unbelief.

Nowadays the Word of God is getting into every place and mankind is running out of excuses. Unwittingly, the world is playing its part in spreading the Word each time it tries to discredit the validity of the Gospel of Jesus Christ. The many discussions and documentaries in the media have created a greater awareness of who Jesus is. Besides, every so often, Hollywood produces yet another movie which brings awareness to the plight of man and the grace of God.

Acts 17:30
And the times of this ignorance God winked at; but now commandeth all men every where to repent:

Repent and Forsake the Sin

The second step in the plan for salvation is repentance, this means to have a complete and thorough change of heart and mind away from evil and toward the Lord. This also means that the individual will forsake the wrongdoings of the past and embrace a new life with God. To be sure, one can only say they have truly repented when they cease to do the thing from which they have repented.

Proverbs 28:13
He that covereth his sins shall not prosper: but whoso confesseth and forsaketh them shall have mercy.

Acts 3:19
Repent ye therefore, and be converted, that your sins may be blotted out, when the times of refreshing shall come from the presence of the Lord;

The Ongoing Message of Repentance

Repentance is vital because it speaks of the sorrow of the heart for the sins that one has committed. It is good to know that the conscience is alive.

2 Corinthians 7:10
For godly sorrow worketh repentance to salvation not to be repented of: but the sorrow of the world worketh death.

Repentance is the message carried on down through the ages and throughout the New Testament. John the Baptist (the forerunner of Jesus Christ) began preaching about repentance.

Matthew 3:1 & 2
1 In those days came John the Baptist, preaching in the wilderness of Judaea,
2 And saying, Repent ye: for the kingdom of heaven is at hand.

Like runners in a relay, Jesus took the baton from John the Baptist and continued preaching about repentance.

Matthew 4:17
From that time Jesus began to preach, and to say, Repent: for the kingdom of heaven is at hand.

Jesus passed the same message onto the apostles.

Acts 2:38
Then Peter said unto them, Repent, and be baptized every one of you in the name of Jesus Christ for the remission of sins, and ye shall receive the gift of the Holy Ghost.

Now it is the responsibility of the Church to preach repentance.

2 Corinthians 5:10 & 11
10 For we must all appear before the judgment seat of Christ; that every one may receive the things done in his body, according to that he hath done, whether it be good or bad.
11 Knowing therefore the terror of the Lord, we persuade men; but we are made manifest unto God; and I trust also are made manifest in your consciences.

Water Baptism

Another step in God's plan for salvation is water baptism. That is, the candidate is totally immersed in water and not just sprinkled as is the practice of some churches.

Mark 16:16
He that believeth and is baptized shall be saved; but he that believeth not shall be damned.

Romans 6:4
Therefore we are buried with him by baptism into death: that like as Christ was raised up from the dead by the glory of the Father, even so we also should walk in newness of life.

Repentance must precede baptism. Actually, during the days of John the Baptist there was even a type of baptism to show that one has repented. It was called, The Baptism of Repentance. In Acts 19 the Apostle Paul met twelve disciples who were baptized unto John's baptism. In other words, they had only repented. The Apostle

Paul, after giving an explanation, baptized them again in the name of Jesus.

> *Acts 19:4 & 5*
> *4 Then said Paul, John verily baptized with the baptism of repentance, saying unto the people, that they should believe on him which should come after him, that is, on Christ Jesus.*
> *5 When they heard this, they were baptized in the name of the Lord Jesus.*

Friend, maybe you, too, were baptized before. If after going through this chapter you see the need to get re-baptized, I urge you to do so. Baptism is not to be taken lightly; it is essential that you are properly baptized. It is part of your plan for salvation.

Putting it all together

In Hebrews 6:1, the Bible speaks of 'repentance from dead works'. When you decided to follow Christ you, in fact, said, "I am no longer willing to live a life of sin. I am going to be dead to sin, and if I am dead to sin, then I cannot respond to its appeal".

> *Romans 6:7*
> *For he that is dead is freed from sin.*

Your decision was based upon what you believed from the Word of God. However, belief is not just a mental acceptance. Belief is demonstrated by action.

> *James 2:17*
> *Even so faith, if it hath not works, is dead, being alone.*

To say that you believe that a particular prescription will work is not the same as taking the medicine. In fact, taking the medicine demonstrates the faith you have in it. If you truly believe in the Lord

Jesus Christ then demonstrate it by going all the way with Him, even in water baptism.

> *Acts 8: 35 - 38*
> *35 Then Philip opened his mouth, and began at the same scripture, and preached unto him Jesus.*
> *36 And as they went on their way, they came unto a certain water: and the eunuch said, See, here is water; what doth hinder me to be baptized?*
> *37 And Philip said, If thou believest with all thine heart, thou mayest. And he answered and said, I believe that Jesus Christ is the Son of God.*
> *38 And he commanded the chariot to stand still: and they went down both into the water, both Philip and the eunuch; and he baptized him.*

CHAPTER SIXTEEN

REASONS FOR WATER BAPTISM

The Mode is a Spiritual Burial

The mode of baptism has been a point of contention among many churches. There have been numerous debates over whether the candidate should be baptized or sprinkled. In the Old Testament Moses sprinkled everyone and everything that had anything to do with the operation of the Tabernacle (Leviticus 8: 10 – 12, 30). And, yes, the sprinkling is a type or shadow of baptism, but when Jesus came He did not get sprinkled; instead John baptized Him in the River Jordan. What Moses did also foreshadowed what we do today when an individual or place is consecrated for a particular ministry, note in the Scriptures below.

> *Acts 13: 2 & 3*
> *2 As they ministered to the Lord, and fasted, the Holy Ghost said, Separate me Barnabas and Saul for the work where-unto I have called them.*
> *3 And when they had fasted and prayed, and laid their hands on them, they sent them away.*

Acts 14:23
And when they had ordained them elders in every church,
and had prayed with fasting, they commended them to the
Lord, on whom they believed.

We are Buried with Christ by Baptism

What do we do with a corpse? Do we sprinkle it with a spoonful of dirt? No we do not, we bury it. Likewise, one who has died to sin must be submerged beneath the waters of baptism symbolizing their spiritual burial.

Romans 6:3 & 4
3 Know ye not, that so many of us as were baptized into
Jesus Christ were baptized into his death?
4 Therefore we are buried with him by baptism into death:
that like as Christ was raised up from the dead by the glory
of the Father, even so we also should walk in newness of
life.

It is part of the New Birth Process

Baptism typifies the burial and resurrection of Jesus. In one sense we are baptized into His death and buried beneath the watery grave. But soon thereafter we are raised up again in the likeness of His resurrection. Additionally, water is essential in the new birth process in much the same way as it is needed in the natural birth process. The baby stays in watery bubble (amniotic sac) during the pregnancy until it is time to be born. That is why to be born again (our spiritual birth) requires us to be also 'born of the water'.

John 3:5
Jesus answered, Verily, verily, I say unto thee, Except a man
be born of water and of the Spirit, he cannot enter into the
kingdom of God.

Christ is Our Example

Jesus is God. He is also the sinless, blameless and spotless Lamb of God. Nevertheless He allowed John the Baptist to baptize Him so we could have an example to follow. If Jesus was baptized we too should be baptized.

Matthew 3:13 - 15
13 Then cometh Jesus from Galilee to Jordan unto John, to be baptized of him.
14 But John forbad him, saying, I have need to be baptized of thee, and comest thou to me?
15 And Jesus answering said unto him, Suffer it to be so now: for thus it becometh us to fulfil all righteousness. Then he suffered him.

Answering of a Good Conscience towards God

Baptism can be likened to the flood in Noah's day which destroyed the evil from off the land. The Scriptures made it clear that the water itself does not take away sin, but it is our conscience that is liberated.

Luke 7:30
But the Pharisees and lawyers rejected the counsel of God against themselves, being not baptized of him.

1 Peter 3:20 & 21
20 Which sometime were disobedient, when once the long-suffering of God waited in the days of Noah, while the ark was a preparing, wherein few, that is, eight souls were saved by water.
21 The like figure whereunto even baptism doth also now save us (not the putting away of the filth of the flesh, but the answer of a good conscience toward God,) by the resurrection of Jesus Christ:

Shadows of Water Baptism from the Old Testament

The rite of water baptism was seen in types and shadows of several of Old Testament stories. Amazingly, even from the Old Testament days, God was preparing the minds of the people for the eventuality of water baptism. Here are a few examples:

- The children of Israel had to pass through the Red Sea (*a type of water baptism involving the blood of Jesus*) when they left Egypt (*indicative of bondage and sin*) but the Egyptians (*sins*) perished in the sea (Exodus 14:26 - 31).
- The prophecy written in Ezekiel 36:25 would have been one that all the Scribes in Jesus' day, should have known. This was perhaps why Jesus was so brunt with Nicodemus, because as a ruler he ought to have known this prophecy in order to understand what Jesus was saying to him (John 3:9 & 10).

Ezekiel 36:25
Then will I sprinkle clean water upon you, and ye shall be clean: from all your filthiness, and from all your idols, will I cleanse you.

The Formula for Water Baptism

What is the formula that should be used while performing this rite? Should one be baptized in the name of Jesus or should it be in the name of the Father, Son & Holy Ghost? Again, there has been much debate over what Peter said in Acts 2:38 and what Jesus commanded in Matthew 28:19. Here is what each Scriptures states:

Matthew 28:19
Go ye therefore, and teach all nations, baptizing them in the name of the Father, and of the Son, and of the Holy Ghost:

Acts 2:38
Then Peter said unto them, Repent, and be baptized every one of you in the name of Jesus Christ for the remission of sins, and ye shall receive the gift of the Holy Ghost.

Some have gone as far as to say that Peter was wrong and all those who followed his instruction are equally wrong. To begin with, let us look at the record found in Matthew chapter 28. Please note that verse 16 says that He met with the eleven disciples (Judas had committed suicide, Matthew 27:5).

Matthew 28:16
Then the eleven disciples went away into Galilee, into a mountain where Jesus had appointed them.

Firstly, Peter got the revelation concerning who Jesus really is, and also received the keys to the kingdom (Matthew 16:13 - 19), so he could speak with confidence on the day of Pentecost (Acts 2).

Secondly, notice how all the following writers promoted the name of the Lord Jesus in their epistles.

Acts 9:29
And he spake boldly in the name of the Lord Jesus, and disputed against the Grecians: but they went about to slay him.

Colossians 3:17
And whatsoever ye do in word or deed, do all in the name of the Lord Jesus, giving thanks to God and the Father by him.

James 5:10
Take, my brethren, the prophets, who have spoken in the name of the Lord, for an example of suffering affliction, and of patience.

His Name is Jesus

Many today are staying clear of denominational titles; Apostolic, Baptist, Church of God, Methodist, Pentecostal, and so on. That could be why a fair number of the new and successful church ministry nowadays characterized themselves as 'Independent' or 'Non-denominational' so as not to get caught up in the controversy, politics or stigma which some denominations carry.

However, the matter of baptism should not be viewed in light of any particular denomination or group. Jesus said it fulfils all righteousness (Matthew 3:15). The Apostle Peter's exhortation in Acts 2:38 concerning baptism in the name of Jesus, is biblically right. It is simply part and parcel of your born again experience.

To be clear, repentance from sin, baptism in Jesus' name, the infilling of the Holy Ghost with the evidence of speaking in other tongues, and living a godly and sober life before God and man, do not make you Apostolic or Pentecostal, or Evangelical, or a member of any other denomination. It simply makes you saved! Praise God. And saved is what we all want to be.

Too often people simply reject these truths for fear of being associated with the denominations that promote them the most. But God's Word cannot be owned, controlled or patented by any one group. It is not exclusive. He is the God of the whole world and everyone has equal access to Him through His Word. This is not to say that you do not attend church; quite the contrary! You need a church for fellowship and spiritual growth but do ensure that you get all that God has for you.

WHY WE BAPTIZE IN JESUS' NAME

Jesus is God's Name in this Present Dispensation

Remember that a spiritual being responds to the name which describes the function it is sent to perform. Throughout the Bible, God used various names which described the various functions He performed from time to time. In this dispensation of grace, God goes by the name Jesus as He procures salvation for His people.

Matthew 1:21
And she shall bring forth a son, and thou shalt call his name
Jesus: for he shall save his people from their sins.

The Disciples Baptized in Jesus' Name

The following references from the book of Acts show that the disciples baptized in the name of Jesus.

Day of Pentecost (2:38 & 41)
Revival in Samaria & the Ethiopian Eunuch (8:12 & 16, 36 - 38)
Cornelius and his household (10:48)
Ephesian Brethren (19:5)
Testimony of the Apostle Paul (22:16)

Jesus is the Pass Code for Heaven

Jesus is the name that guarantees your prayer getting an audience in heaven and we have been instructed to go to the Father in the name of Jesus.

John 16:23
And in that day ye shall ask me nothing. Verily, verily, I say
unto you, Whatsoever ye shall ask the Father in my name, he
will give it you.

The Blood of Jesus is in His Name

At the core of the Christian religion is the belief that Jesus shed His blood on Calvary's cross as a penalty for our sins. When we are baptized in the name of Jesus, it is His blood, and not the water, that washes away our sins. The blood is in His name.

Acts 5:28
Saying, Did not we straitly command you that ye should not
teach in this name? and, behold, ye have filled Jerusalem

with your doctrine, and intend to bring this man's blood upon us.

Remission of Sin is Preached in the Name of Jesus

This is the direct command of the Lord. We are to preach repentance and remission of sins in His name.

Luke 24:47
And that repentance and remission of sins should be preached in his name among all nations, beginning at Jerusalem.

Acts 4:12
Neither is there salvation in any other: for there is none other name under heaven given among men, whereby we must be saved.

Jesus is the Family Name (surname) of Heaven

The family is the basic unit of any society. One can become part of a family through birth, marriage or adoption. All three methods are utilized in God's plan for salvation.

By birth

To become a member of God's family we can have to be born again. To be called a son of God everyone has to go through this new birth process. Jesus had this conversation with Nicodemus (John 3) and told him twice that he had to be born again. Nicodemus' mind was in the natural, but Jesus was describing a spiritual birth.

John 1:12
But as many as received him, to them gave he power to become the sons of God, even to them that believe on his name:

1 John 3:1
Behold, what manner of love the Father hath bestowed upon us, that we should be called the sons of God: therefore the world knoweth us not, because it knew him not.

By marriage

Marriage is an event that requires a lot of planning. On the wedding day the bride wants to look her best for her handsome groom. This special day usually marks the beginning of the newly-weds' life together. As it is in the physical so it is in the spiritual: a spiritual marriage begins the journey between Christ and His bride, the church.

Ephesians 5:25 - 27 & 32
25 Husbands, love your wives, even as Christ also loved the church, and gave himself for it;
26 That he might sanctify and cleanse it with the washing of water by the word,
27 That he might present it to himself a glorious church, not having spot, or wrinkle, or any such thing; but that it should be holy and without blemish.

32 This is a great mystery: but I speak concerning Christ and the church.

Revelation 21:9
And there came unto me one of the seven angels which had the seven vials full of the seven last plagues, and talked with me, saying, Come hither, I will shew thee the bride, the Lamb's wife.

By adoption

Families often adopt other peoples' children as their own. Adoption is one other way we become part of God's family.

Romans 8:15
For ye have not received the spirit of bondage again to fear;
but ye have received the Spirit of adoption, whereby we cry,
Abba, Father.

Ephesians 1:5
Having predestinated us unto the adoption of children by
Jesus Christ to himself, according to the good pleasure of
his will,

Any individual coming into a family using any of the methods I have just described (birth, marriage and adoption) must be willing to take on the family name. Children take the names of their fathers and wives take the name of their husbands. We already know that Jesus is the name of the Son, so His bride and children must have His name.

Ephesians 3:14 & 15
14 For this cause I bow my knees unto the Father of our
Lord Jesus Christ,
15 Of whom the whole family in heaven and earth is named,
...

CHAPTER SEVENTEEN

JESUS, THE CHRIST, REVEALED

✻

Now here is a name that is pretty much well known to all. For some it is the name you utter when you are scared, angry or annoyed. But for the child of God it is the most precious name there is anywhere in this world. The name points to a man Christians claim to be the Son of God. More books, poems, songs, documentaries and columns have been written about Jesus than any other person who walked and will ever walk the face of this earth.

What God did for Adam foreshadowed what Jesus would do for the world [as the world was already in the loins of Adam]. You will recall in the earlier chapters how God substituted an innocent animal to receive the penalty of death in Adam's stead. It is my opinion that the animal implied here is a lamb. Why? Well, the lamb is used many times in the Scripture as the animal of sacrifice (see Genesis 22:8; Exodus 13:13; Leviticus 4:32), plus Jesus is referred to as a lamb.

John 1:29
The next day John seeth Jesus coming unto him, and saith, Behold the Lamb of God, which taketh away the sin of the world.

Revelation 13:8
And all that dwell upon the earth shall worship him, whose names are not written in the book of life of the Lamb slain from the foundation of the world.

According the Scriptures, Jesus Christ was that sinless sacrifice. The virgin birth took care of the inherited and imputed sin, but He was capable of committing sin just as the first Adam. However, He lived a perfect life and thus qualified to be that perfect offering for sin.

The Scripture states: **He knew no sin**.

2 Corinthians 5:21
For he hath made him to be sin for us, who knew no sin; that we might be made the righteousness of God in him.

He did no sin.

1 Peter 2:22
Who did no sin, neither was guile found in his mouth:

There is no sin in Him.

1 John 3:5
And ye know that he was manifested to take away our sins; and in him is no sin.

The Shedding of Blood

The term, shedding of blood, simply means, to kill. Ironically, the One who came to give life had to lose His, because He came to deal with sin. Part of the reason why death follows sin can be seen in the following Scripture:

Hebrews 9:22
And almost all things are by the law purged with blood; and without shedding of blood is no remission.

Death was synonymous with the shedding or spilling of blood (the life of the body), and something has to die for sin to be remitted.

Leviticus 17:11
For the life of the flesh is in the blood: and I have given it to you upon the altar to make an atonement for your souls: for it is the blood that maketh an atonement for the soul.

A Sacrifice for Sins

Suppose we follow the Old Testament practice of substituting an animal to pay for sin, and imagine that we would need to kill an animal, say, a lamb, for each sin committed. I hope you have your calculator handy because that would mean a whole lot of lambs would have to die. And that's only for one person's sins alone. We have not yet begun to tally up other's sins. In this day and age the animal activists would be after the saints.

In the Old Testament when sacrificing animals was the order of the day, God in His mercy allowed the sins of Israel to accumulate for a year. He stayed judgment until the Day of Atonement when Israel, as a nation, would seek national pardon. As you can imagine, this had to be done every year.

Hebrews 9:7
But into the second went the high priest alone once every year, not without blood, which he offered for himself, and for the errors of the people:

Hebrews 9:25
Nor yet that he should offer himself often, as the high priest entereth into the holy place every year with blood of others;

Hebrews 10:3
But in those sacrifices there is a remembrance again made of sins every year.

The Love Factor

Observe also the longsuffering and mercy of God. He kept on blessing and sparing Israel the entire year even though sin was among them. He knew the Day of Atonement was coming and He wanted so much to spare His people. God still wants to spare His people and is not willing to have any should perish.

> *John 3:16 & 17*
> *16 For God so loved the world, that he gave his only begotten Son, that whosoever believeth in him should not perish, but have everlasting life.*
> *17 For God sent not his Son into the world to condemn the world; but that the world through him might be saved.*

Love is the motivating factor behind God's plan for salvation. It is because He loves mankind why He is longsuffering and patient with us.

Jesus the Perfect Sacrifice

As a **dry** sponge has the capacity to absorb more liquid than would a saturated sponge, it certainly would be ideal to use a dry sponge to clean up a spill. Sin certainly was not a small spill. The best person to remove all sin was the One Who is without sin, and that is God Himself. But there was a problem; God is a Spirit and redemption required the shedding of blood, a commodity which a spirit does not have.

> *Luke 24:39*
> *Behold my hands and my feet, that it is I myself: handle me, and see; for a spirit hath not flesh and bones, as ye see me have.*

But God had a plan! He prepared a body and donned it like a suit so He could mingle with humans. This is similar to how a diver would put on special suit so he can survive beneath the water for an extended period of time.

Hebrews 10:5
Wherefore when he cometh into the world, he saith, Sacrifice and offering thou wouldest not, but a body hast thou prepared me:

This body had to be prepared in a way so that it would not come with either inherited or imputed sin. God decided to occasion this through a virgin. Many would say that the virgin birth guaranteed that Jesus would be born sinless; but that is not the case. You see, Mary was also born in sin and had inherited sin, so if Jesus inherited anything from Mary, it too, and He, would contain sin.

But God prepared a body and used a womb, the legal human passage into the earth realm, to step from eternity into time. Mary's womb served as an incubator and no human father was needed because Jesus did not need to be conceived, He is the Everlasting Father.

Isaiah 7:14
Therefore the Lord himself shall give you a sign; Behold, a virgin shall conceive, and bear a son, and shall call his name Immanuel.

Matthew 1:23
Behold, a virgin shall be with child, and shall bring forth a son, and they shall call his name Emmanuel, which being interpreted is, God with us.

Galatians 4:4-5
4 But when the fulness of the time was come, God sent forth his Son, made of a woman, made under the law,
5 To redeem them that were under the law, that we might receive the adoption of sons.

No one else was qualified to die for the sins of the world. If anyone died, it would be for the sins he or she had committed. But when Jesus died, He carried our sins with Him to the cross of Calvary.

Isaiah 53:6
All we like sheep have gone astray; we have turned every one to his own way; and the LORD hath laid on him the iniquity of us all.

Jesus was the perfect man for the job, because he was that spotless lamb that was referred to over and over in the Old Testament. He was foreshadowed as the 'lamb' slain from the foundation of the earth (Revelation 13:8) as a substitute for Adam. He was foreshadowed many times over during the many feasts and offerings the Israelites observed. He was (in a sense) that lamb that was slain in Exodus 12 whose blood was used a protection for the Israelite.

Exodus 12:21-23
21 Then Moses called for all the elders of Israel, and said unto them, Draw out and take you a lamb according to your families, and kill the passover.
22 And ye shall take a bunch of hyssop, and dip it in the blood that is in the bason, and strike the lintel and the two side posts with the blood that is in the bason; and none of you shall go out at the door of his house until the morning.
23 For the LORD will pass through to smite the Egyptians; and when he seeth the blood upon the lintel, and on the two side posts, the LORD will pass over the door, and will not suffer the destroyer to come in unto your houses to smite you.

We know from Scripture that this lamb was to without blemish (representing the sinless and perfect Lamb of God, Jesus), but it was not until we got to the book of the prophet Isaiah that we discovered that the lamb was actually a man (Isaiah 53). It was John the Baptist who finally put a name and face to the man (John 1:29 & 36).

CHAPTER EIGHTEEN

JESUS, GOD IN THE FLESH

There are varying views about who Jesus really is. The worst thing that I have heard is that He really never existed. Others believe He was an actual person but not the God many claimed Him to be. To others, He was simply a good man; a Prophet; or one of several Gods out there or an historical figure whose character was questionable.

Questions abound! Was He married? Did He actually walk the earth? How can One be born of a virgin? Did He, in fact, rise from the dead? Was He caught up on a cloud into Heaven? Is He God? How can God become a man? And is He coming again? Perhaps you have questions of your own!

Matthew 22:41- 43
41 While the Pharisees were gathered together, Jesus asked them,
42 Saying, What think ye of Christ? whose son is he? They say unto him, The son of David.

The answers to the questions above are crucial. Your view of Christ will have a direct impact on how you live your life. There is no middle ground. You either believe or you don't. Hopefully, with the help of the Holy Ghost and the Word of God, you will be convinced that Jesus is real and that He is the Son of God and the Saviour of the world. It is not a good thing to believe otherwise.

John 8:24
I said therefore unto you, that ye shall die in your sins: for if ye believe not that I am he, ye shall die in your sins.

John 20:31
But these are written, that ye might believe that Jesus is the Christ, the Son of God; and that believing ye might have life through his name.

The Bible provides answers to the many questions about Jesus Christ; so the real question is really whether you believe the Bible to be true. Please understand that the Word of God stands; whether we believe it or not.

Romans 3:3- 4
3 For what if some did not believe? shall their unbelief make the faith of God without effect?
4 God forbid: yea, let God be true, but every man a liar; as it is written, That thou mightest be justified in thy sayings, and mightest overcome when thou art judged.

For the record, I believe the Word of God and the record contained therein about Jesus Christ, our Lord. But there are those who do not believe. Long ago, the prophet Isaiah asked this question as he began the prophecy about the Messiah (Lord Jesus Christ) who was to come.

Isaiah 53:1
Who hath believed our report? and to whom is the arm of the LORD revealed?

Getting people to believe in God seems to be the intent and purpose of the entire Bible. That is why it contains information about God, and man, and what happens to those who serve God and those who choose not to serve Him. The writer of Hebrews pointed out that any approach to God must be accompanied by belief in God (Hebrews 11:6).

Spiritually Discerned

The Scripture is clear that we cannot find out God simply by searching (Job 11:7). He is not the kind of Being you can pin down in a corner or monitor in a lab. He is the Almighty God.

Isaiah 40:28
Hast thou not known? hast thou not heard, that the ever-lasting God, the LORD, the Creator of the ends of the earth, fainteth not, neither is weary? there is no searching of his understanding.

It would have been futile to attempt to know God without God's help. In other words, you cannot find out God by learning, but only by discerning, as discerning is spiritual insight.

1 Corinthians 2: 9 - 14
9But as it is written, Eye hath not seen, nor ear heard, neither have entered into the heart of man, the things which God hath prepared for them that love him.
10But God hath revealed them unto us by his Spirit: for the Spirit searcheth all things, yea, the deep things of God.
11For what man knoweth the things of a man, save the spirit of man which is in him? even so the things of God knoweth no man, but the Spirit of God.
12Now we have received, not the spirit of the world, but the spirit which is of God; that we might know the things that are freely given to us of God.
13Which things also we speak, not in the words which man's wisdom teacheth, but which the Holy Ghost teacheth; comparing spiritual things with spiritual.

14But the natural man receiveth not the things of the Spirit of God: for they are foolishness unto him: neither can he know them, because they are spiritually discerned.

Spiritual Revelation

Jesus also wanted to know what people were saying about Him. He wanted to know what His reputation was with the people, so He took a poll one day (Mark 8:27).

Matthew 16:13
When Jesus came into the coasts of Caesarea Philippi, he asked his disciples, saying, Whom do men say that I the Son of man am?

The disciples had lots to say. There were many rumours swirling around the towns and villages about this Rabbi from Galilee (Mark 8:28). Jesus' reputation had preceded Him.

Matthew 16:14
And they said, Some say that thou art John the Baptist: some, Elias; and others, Jeremias, or one of the prophets.

But then He turned the question to them and this time only Peter responded (Mark 8:29). Carefully note the apostle's answer and Jesus' remark.

Matthew 16:16 & 17
16 And Simon Peter answered and said, Thou art the Christ, the Son of the living God.
17 And Jesus answered and said unto him, Blessed art thou, Simon Barjona: for flesh and blood hath not revealed it unto thee, but my Father which is in heaven.

All the other disciples interacted with Jesus in much the same way as Peter did. They heard Him speak on countless occasions (Matthew 7:28 & 29); seen Him tired (John 4:6); watched Him sleep and possibly heard Him snore, too (Matthew 8:24; Mark 4:38). They heard Him pray (Luke 11:1) and saw Him cry (John 11:35). But they all recognized and saw Jesus as just another man; a great Man; a Teacher; Rabbi, even Master.

But Peter got a spiritual revelation. Outside of that revelation Jesus would have been to him the same regular person He had been to everybody else. Hopefully, *As Newborn Babes* will help to you to see clearly that this Jesus is the very God.

Examining the Trinity

The word 'trinity' is not actually found in the Bible but it is used by many denominations to refer to Father, Son and Holy Ghost; the manifestations of God. It is important to view these titles as manifestations of the one true God, rather than individual and separate gods. One reason for the many names of God in the Scriptures is simply the fact that He would change forms to suit the function He wants to fulfill (Hebrews 1:1). Remember, the names depict the functions.

Hebrews 2:14
Forasmuch then as the children are partakers of flesh and blood, he also himself likewise took part of the same; that through death he might destroy him that had the power of death, that is, the devil;

Remember the 100 percent theory we discussed earlier in this book? God (Spirit) was able to tabernacle with man (flesh) through Jesus Christ (the Son of God). Since Jesus had a body He was fully Man but He was also fully God. He was the perfect Mediator since only He alone knew both God and man.

Luke 10:22
All things are delivered to me of my Father: and no man knoweth who the Son is, but the Father; and who the Father is, but the Son, and he to whom the Son will reveal him.

1 Timothy 2:5

For there is one God, and one mediator between God and men, the man Christ Jesus;

Why the Trinity?

The use of the trinity originated during the early church age and was an attempt to explain the Godhead outside of divine revelation. The Scripture does speak of a Father, Son and Holy Ghost, but these are simply manifestations of the one true sovereign God, "*...who is blessed for ever. Amen.*" (Romans 1:25). You see, it is God who manifested Himself in various forms to fulfill various functions but never stopped for once being God. He does not change.

Friend, Jesus is more than the second person in the Trinity. He is the Trinity. He is the Alpha and Omega, the Beginning and the End, the First and the Last (Revelations 22:13), the Author and Finisher of our faith (Hebrews 12:2). He is God in the flesh, and the fullness of the Godhead dwells in Him bodily (Colossians 2:9) bodily. He has always been and will forever be God.

Hebrews 2:9
But we see Jesus, who was made a little lower than the angels for the suffering of death, crowned with glory and honour; that he by the grace of God should taste death for every man.

Jesus, the Father

The term, Father, refers to God is His creative role. St. Matthew recorded that Jesus is the fulfillment of Isaiah's prophecy concerning a Virgin having a Son named Emmanuel, and confirmed that He is 'God with us'. In other words, Jesus is God in the flesh.

John 1:1 & 14
1 In the beginning was the Word, and the Word was with God, and the Word was God.

*14 And the Word was made flesh, and dwelt among us, (and
we beheld his glory, the glory as of the only begotten of the
Father,) full of grace and truth.*

Jesus is the Father, the invisible God, made visible. In other
words, God dressed up in flesh.

2 Corinthians 5:19
*To wit, that God was in Christ, reconciling the world unto
himself, not imputing their trespasses unto them; and hath
committed unto us the word of reconciliation.*

Hebrews 1:3
*Who being the brightness of his glory, and the express image
of his person, and upholding all things by the word of his
power, when he had by himself purged our sins, sat down on
the right hand of the Majesty on high;*

What is the Father's name?

Here is what we know so far: the Father manifested in flesh is
known as the Son (John 1:1 & 14); the Father is in the Son and the
Son is in the Father (John 14:10). The Son's name is Jesus (Matthew
1:21). Since the Father and the Son are one (John 10:30), then their
names will be the same. The disciples knew this and used the name
Jesus whenever they baptized anyone, because Jesus is "...*the name
of the Father, and of the Son, and of the Holy Ghost:*"

Matthew 28:19
*Go ye therefore, and teach all nations, baptizing them in the
name of the Father, and of the Son, and of the Holy Ghost:*

Jesus, the Son

That Jesus is the Son is without debate. He was called Son because
He was not fulfilling a creative role, He came as an extension of God,
the same way a son is the extension of his father. However as Son

of God, it meant He had the same (divine) nature as His Father. He often spoke of His Father and those to whom He spoke knew He was claiming divine status. Take the following passage for instance,

> *John 10:30 - 33*
> *30 I and my Father are one.*
> *31 Then the Jews took up stones again to stone him.*
> *32 Jesus answered them, Many good works have I shewed you from my Father; for which of those works do ye stone me?*
> *33 The Jews answered him, saying, For a good work we stone thee not; but for blasphemy; and because that thou, being a man, makest thyself God.*

The term, Son, refers to the same God, but in His redemptive role. When Jesus spoke of His Father He was referring to His first *form* of manifestation; and since God (the Father) was in Christ, then Jesus (the Son) is everything the Father is (Philippians 2: 6 – 11).

Jesus and the Holy Ghost

It is improper, theologically speaking, to say that God died, for God is a Spirit. Now God, in Spirit form, could not die for our sins for a number of reasons, so a change of form was definitely needed. First of all, they could not see Him. Secondly, you cannot kill a spirit. Thirdly, you cannot kill God. Fourthly, a spirit does not have blood (which is needed to remit sin).

Therefore, in order to redeem mankind, God changed form, manifested Himself in flesh (as Jesus the Christ) for the purpose of death (Hebrews 2:9), became the perfect sacrifice, and died on a cross for our sins and for the sins of the whole world. Natural death occurs when the spirit is released from the body. Likewise, on Calvary's cross, Jesus died, that is, the Spirit left His body.

> *John 14:16 - 18*
> *16 And I will pray the Father, and he shall give you another Comforter, that he may abide with you for ever;*

17 Even the Spirit of truth; whom the world cannot receive, because it seeth him not, neither knoweth him: but ye know him; for he dwelleth with you, and shall be in you.
18 I will not leave you comfortless: I will come to you.

2 Corinthians 3:17
Now the Lord is that Spirit: and where the Spirit of the Lord is, there is liberty.

The key to understanding the Holy Ghost is to remember that each manifestation of God is for a specific function. Do you remember the example we used earlier, in chapter three, involving water? Kindly look at it again. Water can take the form of any container it is in and can exist in liquid, solid (ice) or gaseous state (steam).

If you were thirsty (for instance), would it be prudent for me to offer you a glass of steam? Although steam is water, the form it is in would not serve the purpose. Someone would first have to convert the steam to water before it could quench your thirst, just as God had to change form to satisfy the terms of salvation.

1 Timothy 3:16
And without controversy great is the mystery of godliness: God was manifest in the flesh, justified in the Spirit, seen of angels, preached unto the Gentiles, believed on in the world, received up into glory.

Let us examine the verse above in detail. Please note that the things mentioned in it happened to God.

- Who was manifested in the flesh?

     According St. John 1:1 & 14 it was Jesus who is God manifested in the flesh.

- Who is preached to the Gentiles?

See for yourself. Jesus and His gospel is the subject of preaching to the Gentiles.

Romans 1:16
For I am not ashamed of the gospel of Christ: for it is the power of God unto salvation to every one that believeth; to the Jew first, and also to the Greek.

1 Corinthians 1:23
But we preach Christ crucified, unto the Jews a stumbling-block, and unto the Greeks foolishness;

▪ Who was caught up into glory?

The Scripture in 1Timothy 3:16 above, said it was God, and there is only one God. Jesus is not God also, He is God alone.

Luke 24:51
And it came to pass, while he blessed them, he was parted from them, and carried up into heaven.

Acts 1:9
And when he had spoken these things, while they beheld, he was taken up; and a cloud received him out of their sight.

JESUS IS THE GOD OF THE OLD AND NEW TESTAMENTS

Compare the following Old and New Testament Scriptures.

▪ **He is the 'I Am'**

Exodus 3:14
And God said unto Moses, I AM THAT I AM: and he said, Thus shalt thou say unto the children of Israel, I AM hath sent me unto you.

John 6:35
And Jesus said unto them, I am the bread of life: he that cometh to me shall never hunger; and he that believeth on me shall never thirst.

- **He is the Saviour**

Isaiah 43:11
I, even I, am the LORD; and beside me there is no saviour.

Titus 2:13
Looking for that blessed hope, and the glorious appearing of the great God and our Saviour Jesus Christ;

- **He is the Redeemer**

Isaiah 43:14
Thus saith the LORD, your redeemer, the Holy One of Israel; For your sake I have sent to Babylon, and have brought down all their nobles, and the Chaldeans, whose cry is in the ships.

Titus 2:14
Who gave himself for us, that he might redeem us from all iniquity, and purify unto himself a peculiar people, zealous of good works.

Bearing Witness to Each Other

Finally, each manifestation of God refers to the previous manifestation and confirms, validates or authenticates it. Jesus (the Son) often spoke of His Father (previous manifestation) but promised that when the Holy Ghost comes (the next manifestation), He (the Holy Ghost) will speak of the Son (the previous manifestation).

John 8:54

Jesus answered, If I honour myself, my honour is nothing: it is my Father that honoureth me; of whom ye say, that he is your God:

John 15:26
But when the Comforter is come, whom I will send unto you from the Father, even the Spirit of truth, which proceedeth from the Father, he shall testify of me:

Jesus is God, and He is God alone, for there is only One God. There is none beside, above Him, beneath Him or around Him. He is God all by Himself. There is no contest and no campaign to replace Him. He is not up for election and no one can ever take His place. He was, He is and forever will be God; the King of kings and the Lord of lords. If He is not God of all, then my friend, He is not God at all.

Jude 24-25
24 Now unto him that is able to keep you from falling, and to present you faultless before the presence of his glory with exceeding joy,
25 To the only wise God our Saviour, be glory and majesty, dominion and power, both now and ever. Amen.

CHAPTER NINETEEN

THE DUAL NATURE OF CHRIST

Jesus Christ exhibited two natures; He was both human and divine. You may encounter a few well-meaning folk who may ask you questions like, "If Jesus is the same as the Father, then why did He pray or how come He died?" The answer is simple. Jesus is the embodiment of God in the flesh. In other words, the only time God had a body was in Jesus, the Christ (the Anointed Flesh).

It is in Christ Jesus that the Spirit and the flesh met. This was also what the Tabernacle in the wilderness was showing us. It was in the Tabernacle that God met man; and Jesus is that Tabernacle.

Revelation 21:3
And I heard a great voice out of heaven saying, Behold, the tabernacle of God is with men, and he will dwell with them, and they shall be his people, and God himself shall be with them, and be their God.

In the previous chapter we discovered that Jesus is the manifestation of God in the flesh for the purpose of redemption. He came in bodily form (Jesus, the Son of God) because the flesh has blood and blood was necessary for the remission of sins (Hebrews 9:22). However, only the body, the human side, died. The Spirit, the divine side, never dies.

Ecclesiastes 12:8
Then shall the dust return to the earth as it was: and the spirit shall return unto God who gave it.

Humanity versus Divinity

The Gospel according to Matthew, Mark, Luke and John, are all filled with instances where the two natures of Christ took turns. When one was dominant the other was dormant. For example, as a man, He had to pray, plus He did some things as an example to His disciples. Here are some others.

- **As a man He slept, but as God, He never sleeps**

Mark 4:38
And he was in the hinder part of the ship, asleep on a pillow: and they awake him, and say unto him, Master, carest thou not that we perish?

Psalm 121:3 & 4
3 He will not suffer thy foot to be moved: he that keepeth thee will not slumber.
4 Behold, he that keepeth Israel shall neither slumber nor sleep.

- **As a man He took a ship to get to the other side** (Mark 4:38 above), **but as God he walked on water**

Matthew 14:25
And in the fourth watch of the night Jesus went unto them, walking on the sea.

- **As a man He was fearful of death, but as God He had the power over death**

Matthew 26:39
And he went a little farther, and fell on his face, and prayed, saying, O my Father, if it be possible, let this cup pass from me: nevertheless not as I will, but as thou wilt.

John 10:17 & 18
17 Therefore doth my Father love me, because I lay down my life, that I might take it again.
18 No man taketh it from me, but I lay it down of myself. I have power to lay it down, and I have power to take it again. This commandment have I received of my Father.

John 11:25
Jesus said unto her, I am the resurrection, and the life: he that believeth in me, though he were dead, yet shall he live:

He is both Lord and God

Jesus is Lord and if so, then He is also God (Philippians 2:11).

Psalm 100:3
Know ye that the Lord he is God: it is he that hath made us, and not we ourselves; we are his people, and the sheep of his pasture.

Acts 22:8
And I answered, Who art thou, Lord? [Paul asked] And he said unto me, I am Jesus of Nazareth, whom thou persecutest.

He that is Son is also the Father

Wait a minute — How can one be a father and son at the same time? This is not as mysterious as it sounds. I am a father (praise the Lord) and I am also a son (I got parents and a birth certificate to prove it). If you are a father then you, too, are the son of your parents.

Isaiah 9:6
For unto us a child is born, unto us a son is given: and the government shall be upon his shoulder: and his name shall be called Wonderful, Counseller, The mighty God, The everlasting Father, The Prince of Peace.

God is eternal. He has always been. God has no birthdays. He has no beginning or ending. The '*child*' being '*born*' then obviously refers to the human nature, the flesh. We know Jesus was born "*... in Bethlehem of Judaea in the days of Herod the king ...*" (Matthew 2:1): Not sure if it was on December 25th, but for sure He was born.

But the '*son being given*" calls the divine into question, for "*God so loved the world that He gave His only begotten Son...*" (St. John 3:16). And if you doubt Isaiah words, Jesus affirms the same:

John 14:9
Jesus saith unto him, Have I been so long time with you, and yet hast thou not known me, Philip? he that hath seen me hath seen the Father; and how sayest thou then, Shew us the Father?

Can I get a Witness?

Here are a few people from the Scriptures who found out that Jesus is God.

- Stephen, even in while dying, claimed Jesus as God.

Acts 7:59
And they stoned Stephen, calling upon God, and saying, Lord Jesus, receive my spirit.

- The writer of Hebrews agrees:

Hebrews 1:8
But unto the Son he saith, Thy throne, O God, is for ever and ever: a sceptre of righteousness is the sceptre of thy kingdom.

What does the Master have to say?

Jesus' own words attest to who He is. He will not deny Himself even in the face of death. Please read the following Scriptures slowly and carefully. Make no mistake about it: Jesus is the One Lord, the only wise God and Saviour.

John 8:58
Jesus said unto them, Verily, verily, I say unto you, Before Abraham was, I am.

John 10:30
I and my Father are one.

John 12:45
And he that seeth me seeth him that sent me.

God fulfilled the function of redemption by manifesting Himself as the Son of God and dying on a cross for our sins. It was God that was in Christ reconciling the world unto Himself (2 Corinthians 5:19). Therefore, the Son's main duty was to point us to the Father.

John 14:6
Jesus saith unto him, I am the way, the truth, and the life: no man cometh unto the Father, but by me.

Jesus, then, is the Door (John 10:9), the way to God (John 14:6), and the Mediator.

1 Timothy 2:5
For there is one God, and one mediator between God and men, the man Christ Jesus;

1 Timothy 4:10
For therefore we both labour and suffer reproach, because we trust in the living God, who is the Saviour of all men, specially of those that believe.

CHAPTER TWENTY

THE WORK OF
THE HOLY GHOST

The terms 'Holy Ghost' and 'Holy Spirit' are one and the same. The New Testament writers were inspired to use Ghost to refer to the 'Spirit in motion'. But who or what is the Holy Spirit? Well, recall what you know about God — He is a Spirit and He is holy. So right away, we know that the Holy Spirit must be God.

John 4:24
God is a Spirit: and they that worship him must worship him
in spirit and in truth.

One of the characteristics of a spirit is that it is invisible. We know that God is a Spirit. Therefore, no man has seen God in His spirit form, because He is invisible. The Scripture backs this up:

John 1:18
No man hath seen God at any time; the only begotten Son,
which is in the bosom of the Father, he hath declared him.

But when we see Jesus we are in fact seeing the Father. In the previous chapter recall what Jesus said about seeing the Father when you see Him (John 14:9); He is the image of the invisible God (Colossians 1:15).

The Holy Ghost is the Father

We have already established that the Holy Ghost is God. Therefore, technically, the Holy Ghost is also the Father, though the roles are different. We can therefore conclude that the Holy Ghost, from a redemptive relationship point of view, is also the Father of Jesus Christ. The Scripture points out that when Mary wanted to how she was going to conceive without a man this is the answer she received:

> *Luke 1:35*
> *And the angel answered and said unto her, The Holy Ghost shall come upon thee, and the power of the Highest shall overshadow thee: therefore also that holy thing which shall be born of thee shall be called the Son of God.*

The Holy Ghost is Jesus

We have also recently pointed out in the previous chapter that a ghost is a personified spirit. In other words, we know where that spirit comes from. Jesus promised to send *another comforter*, and in speaking of the Holy Ghost, had this to say:

> *John 14:18*
> *I will not leave you comfortless: I will come to you.*

Please look carefully at the verse notice how He reveals who the other Comforter will be. Jesus said, "*I will come to you*". Wait, there is more.

> *1 Corinthians 15:45*
> *And so it is written, The first man Adam was made a living soul; the last Adam was made a quickening spirit.*

> *2 Corinthians 3:17*
> *Now the Lord is that Spirit: and where the Spirit of the Lord is, there is liberty.*

THE MINISTRY OF THE HOLY GHOST

Each manifestation of God is for a specific purpose so let us examine the purpose of the Holy Ghost. The Holy Ghost is God in His supportive and empowerment role.

The Holy Ghost helps us to keep the Word of the Lord.

The Holy Ghost brings things back to our remembrance and reminds us of what God said in His Word.

Ezekiel 36:27
And I will put my spirit within you, and cause you to walk in my statutes, and ye shall keep my judgments, and do them.

John 14:26
But the Comforter, which is the Holy Ghost, whom the Father will send in my name, he shall teach you all things, and bring all things to your remembrance, whatsoever I have said unto you.

The Holy Ghost helps us to understand the Bible.

The things about God are not always easily understood, but the Holy Spirit is given to us to help illuminate the Scriptures, that is, to help us understand the things which God has revealed (1 Corinthians 2:10, 12 - 14).

John 16:13
Howbeit when he, the Spirit of truth, is come, he will guide you into all truth: for he shall not speak of himself; but whatsoever he shall hear, that shall he speak: and he will shew you things to come.

1 John 2:27
But the anointing which ye have received of him abideth in you, and ye need not that any man teach you: but as the same

anointing teacheth you of all things, and is truth, and is no lie, and even as it hath taught you, ye shall abide in him.

The Holy Ghost reproves.

Most businesses have their premises monitored around the clock for security purposes, during regular time but especially during non-business hours. When the alarms goes off security personnel flock to the site to investigate and report their findings. The Holy Spirit functions in a way similar to the alarm. He signals when anything threatens your stance with God.

John 16:7 - 11
7 Nevertheless I tell you the truth; It is expedient for you that I go away: for if I go not away, the Comforter will not come unto you; but if I depart, I will send him unto you.
8 And when he is come, he will reprove the world of sin, and of righteousness, and of judgment:
9 Of sin, because they believe not on me;
10 Of righteousness, because I go to my Father, and ye see me no more;
11 Of judgment, because the prince of this world is judged.

The Holy Ghost sanctifies.

God is a Holy God. Through the ministry of the Holy Ghost He selects, sanctifies, appoints and equips those whom He wants to work in His kingdom for His own glory.

Psalms 4:3
But know that the LORD hath set apart him that is godly for himself: the LORD will hear when I call unto him.

Romans 15:16
That I should be the minister of Jesus Christ to the Gentiles, ministering the gospel of God, that the offering up of the

Gentiles might be acceptable, being sanctified by the Holy Ghost.

Acts 13:2
As they ministered to the Lord, and fasted, the Holy Ghost said, Separate me Barnabas and Saul for the work where-unto I have called them.

The Holy Ghost empowers for specific purposes.

Each Spirit-filled believer is entrusted with the responsibility of winning another soul to Christ. One of the functions of the Holy Ghost is to empower us to be witnesses for Christ.

Acts 1:8
But ye shall receive power, after that the Holy Ghost is come upon you: and ye shall be witnesses unto me both in Jerusalem, and in all Judaea, and in Samaria, and unto the uttermost part of the earth.

Scriptural Representations

Throughout the Scriptures different emblems have been used to represent the Holy Spirit.

1. A lamp or fire; because they give light in darkness, they reveal
2. The anointing oil; used to denote a mark of calling
3. The dove; as in the case of Jesus' baptism, a symbol of hope and peace

ANOTHER QUICK ASSIGNMENT

Try to locate scriptural references for the representations above. Feel free to add to the lists, and highlight which of them is most widely used in the Scriptures.

CHAPTER TWENTY ONE

THE GIFT OF THE HOLY GHOST

The Holy Ghost plays an important and vital part in the new birth process and also in the operations of the church, the body of Christ. Jesus told Nicodemus that he must be born of the water and of the Spirit.

John 3:5 - 8
5 Jesus answered, Verily, verily, I say unto thee, Except a man be born of water and of the Spirit, he cannot enter into the kingdom of God.
6 That which is born of the flesh is flesh; and that which is born of the Spirit is spirit.
7 Marvel not that I said unto thee, Ye must be born again.
8 The wind bloweth where it listeth, and thou hearest the sound thereof, but canst not tell whence it cometh, and whither it goeth: so is every one that is born of the Spirit.

The Quickening Sound

The Holy Spirit is the life of the child of God. Many would-be mothers have endured still births, but what a joy it is when the signs of life (sound and movement) are present. God, in His sovereign will, has chosen tongues (a sound) to signify that new life in the newborn child of God.

Acts 2:4
And they were all filled with the Holy Ghost, and began to speak with other tongues, as the Spirit gave them utterance.

Romans 8:11
But if the Spirit of him that raised up Jesus from the dead dwell in you, he that raised up Christ from the dead shall also quicken your mortal bodies by his Spirit that dwelleth in you.

Baptisms in Water and by the Spirit

Notice carefully what Jesus said; the born again process includes baptisms in water and by the Spirit. On the day of Pentecost the Apostle Peter, the one who got the keys to the Kingdom, (Matthew 16:19), made sure he included this fact in his response to the question of the day. This is a non-negotiable truth.

Acts 2:37 & 38
37 Now when they heard this, they were pricked in their heart, and said unto Peter and to the rest of the apostles, Men and brethren, what shall we do?
38 Then Peter said unto them, Repent, and be baptized every one of you in the name of Jesus Christ for the remission of sins, and ye shall receive the gift of the Holy Ghost.

The order in which one experiences these two aspects of the new birth is irrelevant as long as they both occur. The Scriptures make it clear that some people receive the Holy Ghost before water baptism in the name of Jesus, while the order is reversed for others. Check out these few examples from the Word of God.

- John the Baptist received the Holy Ghost from his mother's womb (Luke 1:15) yet he knew he needed to be baptized (Matthew 3:14).
- Cornelius received the Holy Ghost prior to being baptized (Acts 10:44 - 48).

- The disciples from Ephesus received the Holy Ghost after Paul baptized them in the name of the Lord Jesus (Acts 19:5 & 6). They had been baptized before but not in Jesus' name.

How to Receive the Holy Ghost

Have you received the Holy Ghost since you believed? Friend, God wants to fill you up with Himself. That is right: He wants to dwell in you by His Spirit today. This is not only for the saints of old as is taught by some, it is for us today.

Acts 2:39
For the promise is unto you, and to your children, and to all that are afar off, even as many as the Lord our God shall call.

Ephesians 5:18
And be not drunk with wine, wherein is excess; but be filled with the Spirit;

Take a look around today; do you see what is happening in our world? If anybody needed the Spirit of God, I would vote for the saints of today. You see, you and I can never, by our own will and power, fulfill the will of God. God has come to live in us (by His Spirit) to teach us how to please Him and work out His purpose in our lives.

Philippians 2:13
For it is God which worketh in you both to will and to do of his good pleasure.

Romans 8:14
For as many as are led by the Spirit of God, they are the sons of God.

Ask for the Holy Ghost

If you have truly repented of your sins and are baptized in water in the name of Jesus, God promised to give the Holy Ghost to you and all of His children who come to Him. So go ahead and ask Him today, knowing and believing in your heart that God wants you filled with His Spirit.

Luke 11:13
If ye then, being evil, know how to give good gifts unto your children: how much more shall your heavenly Father give the Holy Spirit to them that ask him?

Believe on the Lord Jesus

It is through faith that we receive anything from God. Without faith we get nothing. So believe on Him today; He is faithful to perform what He promised.

John 7:37 & 38
37 In the last day, that great day of the feast, Jesus stood and cried, saying, If any man thirst, let him come unto me, and drink.
38 He that believeth on me, as the scripture hath said, out of his belly shall flow rivers of living water.

Speak as the Spirit Gives Utterance

Many today have not yet received the Holy Ghost and perhaps this is due to what they think must accompany their infilling. The Word of God indicates that the believer will speak in tongues as the Spirit gives the utterance. That's it.

Acts 2:4
And they were all filled with the Holy Ghost, and began to speak with other tongues, as the Spirit gave them utterance.

Note, it is you, the receiving believer, who does the speaking; so believe God for the gift of the Holy Ghost and say, in faith, the utterances on your tongue.

Romans 10:8
But what saith it? The word is nigh thee, even in thy mouth, and in thy heart: that is, the word of faith, which we preach;

Join the thousands today who are filled full of the Spirit of God; it is totally Biblical. Check out this impressive list:

Luke 1:41
And it came to pass, that, when Elisabeth heard the salutation of Mary, the babe leaped in her womb; and Elisabeth was filled with the Holy Ghost:

Luke 1:67
And his father Zacharias was filled with the Holy Ghost, and prophesied, saying,

Acts 4:8
Then Peter, filled with the Holy Ghost, said unto them, Ye rulers of the people, and elders of Israel,

Acts 13:9
Then Saul, (who also is called Paul,) filled with the Holy Ghost, set his eyes on him,

Evidences of the Holy Ghost

God in His Sovereignty chose to operate by speech or by His Word. He created the heaven and earth by speaking. All He said was, "*Let there be...*" and there was. Even though man was not created by speech, but created from the dust of the earth, this creation was preceded by speech (Genesis 1:26 & 27). Besides, if we were to get a little technical, we could argue that man was in fact created by the Word — which is God, according John 1:1 & 3.

Psalm 33:9
For he spake, and it was done; he commanded, and it stood fast.

As a result, God recognizes and responds to speech, especially when it is directed towards Him. That is perhaps why God reacts to and encourages prayer and praise. He promises to respond to these, as they are most often verbal.

2 Chronicles 7:14
If my people, which are called by my name, shall humble themselves, and pray, and seek my face, and turn from their wicked ways; then will I hear from heaven, and will forgive their sin, and will heal their land.

Psalm 22:3
But thou art holy, O thou that inhabitest the praises of Israel.

Let us look at a few more examples from the Word of God:

Exodus 6:5
And I have also heard the groaning of the children of Israel, whom the Egyptians keep in bondage; and I have remembered my covenant.

Psalm 34:6
This poor man cried, and the LORD heard him, and saved him out of all his troubles.

2 Chronicles 5:13 & 14
13 It came even to pass, as the trumpeters and singers were as one, to make one sound to be heard in praising and thanking the LORD; and when they lifted up their voice with the trumpets and cymbals and instruments of musick, and praised the LORD, saying, For he is good; for his mercy endureth for

*ever: that then the house was filled with a cloud, even the
house of the LORD;*
*14 So that the priests could not stand to minister by reason
of the cloud: for the glory of the LORD had filled the house
of God.*

Jeremiah 33:3
*Call unto me, and I will answer thee, and shew thee great
and mighty things, which thou knowest not.*

The Issue of Speaking in Tongues

Now that we have established the fact that God often acts by,
encourages and responds to speech, let us examine the issue of
tongues. God has chosen to use 'speaking in tongues' as the initial
evidence that one is filled with the Holy Ghost. Now, not everyone
who speaks with tongues is filled with the Holy Ghost (there are
actors and deceivers everywhere except in heaven); but everyone
who is filled with the Spirit of God must speak in tongues as the
initial evidence. As always we have proof from the Scripture.

Acts 2:4
*And they were all filled with the Holy Ghost, and began to
speak with other tongues, as the Spirit gave them utterance.*

Acts 10:44-46
*44 While Peter yet spake these words, the Holy Ghost fell on
all them which heard the word.*
*45 And they of the circumcision which believed were aston-
ished, as many as came with Peter, because that on the
Gentiles also was poured out the gift of the Holy Ghost.*
*46 For they heard them speak with tongues, and magnify
God*

The Scriptures say that on the Day of Pentecost cloven tongues
of fire sat upon the 120 saints (Acts 1:15) that were gathered in the
Upper Room when God poured out His Spirit.

Acts 2:3
And there appeared unto them cloven tongues like as of fire, and it sat upon each of them.

The word 'cloven' means 'two'. So, on that day the disciples manifested two types of tongues. Again, we go to the Word of God for clarity on what those two types of tongues should be.

1 Corinthians 13:1
Though I speak with the tongues of men and of angels, and have not charity, I am become as sounding brass, or a tinkling cymbal.

Tongues of Men

As the disciples spoke in tongues on the Day of Pentecost, visitors from other countries could understand what they were saying (Acts 2:6 – 11). The disciples were supernaturally enabled to speak in another earthly language. In other words, they were speaking *"tongues of men"*. Someone who knows that language can translate these types of tongues. So when you speak in tongues you could be speaking Italian or Spanish (or any other language) and not know it; but someone who speaks that language would know what you are saying.

Tongues of Angels

Not all tongues can be traced to another country on Earth. As you speak in tongues you could be speaking a heavenly language. The Bible calls this phenomenon, *tongues of angels.*

1 Corinthians 14:2
For he that speaketh in an unknown tongue speaketh not unto men, but unto God: for no man understandeth him; howbeit in the spirit he speaketh mysteries.

The gift of interpretation is necessary in order to understand and interpret tongues of angels.

1 Corinthians 14:27 - 28
27 If any man speak in an unknown tongue, let it be by two, or at the most by three, and that by course; and let one interpret.
28 But if there be no interpreter, let him keep silence in the church; and let him speak to himself, and to God.

The Gift of Tongues

It is important here to make a distinction between the speaking in tongues as the initial evidence of being filled with (or receiving the gift of) the Holy Ghost, and speaking tongues as a spiritual gift. The Spirit gives diverse gifts (spiritual gifts) to the Church, such as the body of Christ, for the effective administration and operation of the ministry.

1 Corinthians 12:1, 4, 7 - 11
1 Now concerning spiritual gifts, brethren, I would not have you ignorant.

4 Now there are diversities of gifts, but the same Spirit.

7 But the manifestation of the Spirit is given to every man to profit withal.
8 For to one is given by the Spirit the word of wisdom; to another the word of knowledge by the same Spirit;
9 To another faith by the same Spirit; to another the gifts of healing by the same Spirit;
10 To another the working of miracles; to another prophecy; to another discerning of spirits; to another divers kinds of tongues; to another the interpretation of tongues:
11 But all these worketh that one and the selfsame Spirit, dividing to every man severally as he will.

The spiritual gift of *'divers kinds of tongues'* (vs. 10) is a super-natural ability to speak in different languages or unknown tongues, whether of *men* or of *angels*. The audience hearing the tongues must be able to understand what is being said (edified). If the general audience does not speak the language spoken 'in tongues', and no one else is present who speaks that particular language, someone with the spiritual gift of *'interpretation of tongues'* will be needed to translate.

The Fruit of the Spirit

Speaking in tongues is not the only evidence that a saint has been filled with the Holy Ghost. It is, however, the initial evidence. The believer must go on to developing and displaying the fruit of the Spirit by allowing the Holy Ghost to work on the inner man to produce Christ-like traits.

Galatians 5:22 & 23
22 But the fruit of the Spirit is love, joy, peace, longsuffering, gentleness, goodness, faith,
23 Meekness, temperance: against such there is no law.

The fruit of the Spirit will identify a true believer; one who is destined for everlasting life. The type of fruit will determine which spirit is indwelling and influencing that person's life.

Matthew 7:18 - 20
18 A good tree cannot bring forth evil fruit, neither can a corrupt tree bring forth good fruit.
19 Every tree that bringeth not forth good fruit is hewn down, and cast into the fire.
20 Wherefore by their fruits ye shall know them.

Yes friend, a Spirit-filled life must be a fruitful life and vice versa. We simply cannot produce the fruit of the Spirit without the Holy Ghost and the Word of God. Here is how the Master Jesus said it:

John 15:4 - 6

4 Abide in me, and I in you. As the branch cannot bear fruit of itself, except it abide in the vine; no more can ye, except ye abide in me.

5 I am the vine, ye are the branches: He that abideth in me, and I in him, the same bringeth forth much fruit: for without me ye can do nothing.

6 If a man abide not in me, he is cast forth as a branch, and is withered; and men gather them, and cast them into the fire, and they are burned.

The fruit of the Spirit must be constantly seen in the believer's life; and like any other fruit, it will take time to achieve perfection.

John 15:16

Ye have not chosen me, but I have chosen you, and ordained you, that ye should go and bring forth fruit, and that your fruit should remain: that whatsoever ye shall ask of the Father in my name, he may give it you.

2 Peter 1:5 - 8

5 And beside this, giving all diligence, add to your faith virtue; and to virtue knowledge;

6 And to knowledge temperance; and to temperance patience; and to patience godliness;

7 And to godliness brotherly kindness; and to brotherly kindness charity.

8 For if these things be in you, and abound, they make you that ye shall neither be barren nor unfruitful in the knowledge of our Lord Jesus Christ.

Dear Friend, as a fellow Christian believer, is your life a fertile garden for the things of the Spirit of God? Are the fruit and gifts of the Spirit evident in your life? If you are not as fruitful as the Word of God says you should be, then, my friend, it is time to break up your fallow ground, root out those weeds, and plant some good seeds.

Hosea 10:12
Sow to yourselves in righteousness, reap in mercy; break up your fallow ground: for it is time to seek the LORD, till he come and rain righteousness upon you.

CHAPTER TWENTY TWO

A NEW CREATURE IN CHRIST

Well, praise the Lord! We are new creatures in Christ Jesus. The day you got saved, you were born again. That is, if you have trusted Christ as your personal Saviour, repented of your sins, and were baptized in water in the name of Jesus and received the precious gift of the Holy Ghost with the initial evidence of speaking in tongues, and are living a godly life before God, then the Bible says that you are saved.

Perhaps you are saying to yourself, I know I am different because I sense a change in my desires, convictions, beliefs and ambitions. I find myself longing for the salvation of my friends and family members. I find myself interested in spiritual and eternal things and I love to fellowship with the saints "...*that have obtained like precious faith with us through the righteousness of God and our Saviour Jesus Christ:*" (2 Peter 1:1). Friend, those feelings and other thoughts you may and will have, are among the strong sentiments you will encounter when you are truly born again. You should also know that you are a miracle. Whatever your current age might be; you have experienced a new birth.

2 Corinthians 5:17
Therefore if any man be in Christ, he is a new creature: old things are passed away; behold, all things are become new.

WHAT DOES IT MEAN TO BE A NEW CREATURE?

This means you are like a little baby just coming into the kingdom of God. You are in diapers my friend; you have started life over with a clean slate. As a result, there are some things you should know about your new status.

You are now a child of God.

Yes you. God has adopted us into His family (Ephesians 1:5). You have been born again (1 Peter 1:23). You have a new name written down in glory (Revelation 2:17); they might as well start calling you God's little son or daughter. You are the King's kid.

1 Peter 2:9
But ye are a chosen generation, a royal priesthood, an holy nation, a peculiar people; that ye should shew forth the praises of him who hath called you out of darkness into his marvellous light:

1 John 3:2
Beloved, now are we the sons of God, and it doth not yet appear what we shall be: but we know that, when he shall appear, we shall be like him; for we shall see him as he is.

You are now an heir of God and all the promises of the Bible are yours to claim and enjoy.

Romans 8:16
The Spirit itself beareth witness with our spirit, that we are the children of God:

1 John 3:2
Beloved, now are we the sons of God, and it doth not yet appear what we shall be: but we know that, when he shall appear, we shall be like him; for we shall see him as he is.

You are not perfect.

I hate to burst your bubble so quickly after all that talk about being the King's kid and all, but too many believers become disheartened with their own shortcomings.

2 Peter 3:17-18
17 Ye therefore, beloved, seeing ye know these things before, beware lest ye also, being led away with the error of the wicked, fall from your own stedfastness.
18 But grow in grace, and in the knowledge of our Lord and Saviour Jesus Christ. To him be glory both now and for ever. Amen.

The Master did the same thing to the Apostle Peter, "*For whom the Lord loveth he chasteneth, and scourgeth every son whom he receiveth...*" (Hebrews 12:6). Shortly after acknowledging Jesus as "*...the Christ, the Son of the living God ...*" (Matthew 16:16), Peter got one right between the eyes when later down in the same chapter Jesus "*... turned, and said unto Peter, Get thee behind me, Satan: thou art an offence unto me: for thou savourest not the things that be of God, but those that be of men ...*"(Matthew 16:23). Such a rebuke will sober up anybody lest they become proud and haughty.

Do not expect to be perfect overnight either. Nobody is perfect. Your born again experience is a new birth; which means you are a babe in Christ. There are some things which you will learn and re-learn, so keep practicing doing the right things. Practice makes improvement. Only God is perfect.

1 Peter 2:1-3
1 Wherefore laying aside all malice, and all guile, and hypoc-risies, and envies, and all evil speakings,
2 As newborn babes, desire the sincere milk of the word, that ye may grow thereby:
3 If so be ye have tasted that the Lord is gracious.

You are a recipient of God's best gift.

Know also that you have received the precious gift of salvation by faith. Jesus paid the price by dying on a cruel cross for all your sins. You simply cannot top that gift!

Ephesians 2:8 & 9
8 For by grace are ye saved through faith; and that not of yourselves: it is the gift of God:
9 Not of works, lest any man should boast.

The God of heaven and earth has forgiven all of your sins. This is a wonderful and marvelous gift.

1 John 1:9
If we confess our sins, he is faithful and just to forgive us our sins, and to cleanse us from all unrighteousness.

You are justified.

When you are born again, you are given a fresh start with God. The Bible calls that justification. When Adam and Eve were created, they were created completely sinless. However, they were capable of sinning, and they did sin.

However, because of the Christ's sacrifice, as a new creature in Christ I am justified in God's eyes. In other words, God sees me *just-as-if-I'd* (justified) never sinned. I am a brand new creature in Christ.

Romans 5:1
Therefore being justified by faith, we have peace with God through our Lord Jesus Christ:

Galatians 6:15
For in Christ Jesus neither circumcision availeth any thing, nor uncircumcision, but a new creature.

You took off the old man and put on the new man.

The term, old man, refers to our sinful nature and practices. Once we become a born again Christian, we must seek to have a new way of life. We have a new man living on the inside. He is the Holy Spirit of God, "*...Christ in you, the hope of glory...*" (Colossians 1:27). Things, places and conversations which are not in keeping with a sanctified and holy lifestyle must be avoided at all cost.

Ephesians 4:22 - 24
22 That ye put off concerning the former conversation the old man, which is corrupt according to the deceitful lusts;
23 And be renewed in the spirit of your mind;
24 And that ye put on the new man, which after God is created in righteousness and true holiness.

1 Thessalonians 4:3 - 6
3 For this is the will of God, even your sanctification, that ye should abstain from fornication:
4 That every one of you should know how to possess his vessel in sanctification and honour;
5 Not in the lust of concupiscence, even as the Gentiles which know not God:

6 That no man go beyond and defraud his brother in any matter: because that the Lord is the avenger of all such, as we also have forewarned you and testified.

You are now a target.

Know for sure there will be times of testing and temptation. You may even make mistakes, but remember you can always go to God to make it right (1 John 1:9; 2:1). Do not let the evil one tell you that you cannot be forgiven. God is faithful to forgive. The evil one may even try to tell you that you should not be struggling to do the right thing and that doing the right thing should always come naturally since you are a Christian, but resist such argument.

Sure we are required to grow and mature as times goes on. We should not be in diapers all life long. But a struggle is a struggle, and not all struggles are the same. Some struggles have their roots in things of the past which may take spiritual warfare to break (Mark 9:29). Therefore, before you start beating yourself, kindly take a moment to read Romans 7 and the Apostle Paul will tell you of his own struggles.

Your walk and socializing patterns must change.

When I speak of your 'walk', I am not referring to the motion of moving on foot, using the feet alternately to advance in a particular direction. Instead, I am referring particularly to the manner in which you conduct yourself as you go through life. Your walk is a conversation. It says something about who you are and the God you serve; Whose you are.

Ephesians 5:8 & 11
8 For ye were sometimes darkness, but now are ye light in the Lord: walk as children of light:

11 And have no fellowship with the unfruitful works of darkness, but rather reprove them.

CHAPTER TWENTY THREE

PRAISE, WORSHIP AND PRAYER

The early days of your new life in Christ are crucial times. During these early years it is important for you to be well nourished and protected, much like you would a newborn child. Those who are involved in nurturing new converts know that special care and patience are required as they grow up to become "...*strong in the Lord, and in the power of his might* ... (Ephesians 6:10).

The Bible itself is a package (ingredients) of spiritual food for the growing Christian and it is filled with the guidelines (menu) and nutrients that will serve as vital nourishment to help you on your spiritual journey. I hope you are ready because I am excited to show you more examples from the Word of God to help you on your way.

Ephesians 4:15
But speaking the truth in love, may grow up into him in all things, which is the head, even Christ:

Praise and Worship

I believe one of the first things we ought to teach new converts is praising God. I mean, to know that your life was spared until you got saved is enough to make you want to worship God. Countless number of lost souls did not get a second chance to say, "Lord, have mercy", and here you are now sweetly, after perhaps doing the some of very same things.

> *1 Corinthians 6:11*
> *And such were some of you: but ye are washed, but ye are sanctified, but ye are justified in the name of the Lord Jesus, and by the Spirit of our God.*

Praising God is not an option.

Every living being is commanded to praise God (Psalm 150:6).

> *Psalm 115:17*
> *The dead praise not the LORD, neither any that go down into silence.*

> *Psalm 150:6*
> *Let every thing that hath breath praise the LORD. Praise ye the LORD.*

True worshippers are in high demand.

> *John 4:23-24*
> *23 But the hour cometh, and now is, when the true worshippers shall worship the Father in spirit and in truth: for the Father seeketh such to worship him.*
> *24 God is a Spirit: and they that worship him must worship him in spirit and in truth.*

BENEFITS FOR BEING A TRULY SINCERE WORSHIPPER

God delivers the worshipper (Acts 16: 25 & 26).

> *Psalm 142:7*
> *Bring my soul out of prison, that I may praise thy name: the righteous shall compass me about; for thou shalt deal bountifully with me.*

God heals the worshipper (Isaiah 38).

Isaiah 38:18
For the grave cannot praise thee, death can not celebrate thee: they that go down into the pit cannot hope for thy truth.

God hears the worshipper.

John 9:31
Now we know that God heareth not sinners: but if any man be a worshipper of God, and doeth his will, him he heareth.

God responds to worshippers.

1 Samuel 30:7 & 8
7 And David said to Abiathar the priest, Ahimelech's son, I pray thee, bring me hither the ephod. And Abiathar brought thither the ephod to David.
8 And David inquired at the LORD, saying, Shall I pursue after this troop? shall I overtake them? And he answered him, Pursue: for thou shalt surely overtake them, and without fail recover all.

A GOOD PRAYER LIFE

We communicate to God through prayer. Prayer is something you need to learn to do. Babies learn to speak by observing, listening and interacting with others. Plus there are times when we deliberately teach them specific words.

When our children were much younger, I can recall hearing my wife (with that teacher to student tone) teach them words like, "No", "Danger", "Dadda", (my personal favourite), "Mamma", plus the so-called magic words, "Please" and "Thank You". Similarly, the convert must learn how to pray.

I found it very encouraging that the only thing the disciples asked Jesus to teach them was *'how to pray'*. So ask your pastor or teacher to teach you how to pray.

Luke 11:1
And it came to pass, that, as he was praying in a certain place, when he ceased, one of his disciples said unto him, Lord, teach us to pray, as John also taught his disciples.

In response to the disciples' request the Lord Jesus gave the following prayer (commonly known as the Lord's Prayer) as a model. Many people can quote it, but few take the time to really understand it. It is a model, because the disciples wanted to know '*how to*' pray.

Matthew 6:9 - 13
9 After this manner therefore pray ye:
Our Father which art in heaven, Hallowed be thy name.
10 Thy kingdom come. Thy will be done in earth, as it is in heaven.
11 Give us this day our daily bread.
12 And forgive us our debts, as we forgive our debtors.
13 And lead us not into temptation, but deliver us from evil: For thine is the kingdom, and the power, and the glory, for ever. Amen.

As you examine the Lord's Prayer you will find the following principles in it:

1. Begin and end your prayer with praise.
2. Put God's will and Kingdom before your personal agenda.
3. Pray everyday.
4. Do not just pray for yourself. Notice the '*us*' and the '*our*' in the model prayer.
5. Ask for forgiveness and guidance. Note that you will receive forgiveness if you forgive those who have wronged you.
6. Say, 'Amen'. In other words, close on a positive note. The word '*Amen*' means, "It is so". So when you pray, believe that God hears and will answer your prayer.

Hebrews 11:6
But without faith it is impossible to please him: for he that cometh to God must believe that he is, and that he is a rewarder of them that diligently seek him.

<small>KEYS TO A SUCCESSFUL PRAYER LIFE</small>

Set aside a time and private place for prayer and stick to it.

Jesus had a particular spot that His disciples knew about. I also have a little spot in my house where I pray early in the mornings. My family knows to be quiet in that spot at certain times of the mornings.

Luke 22: 39 & 41
And he came out, and went, as he was wont, to the mount of Olives; and his disciples also followed him.

41 And he was withdrawn from them about a stone's cast, and kneeled down, and prayed,

John 18:1 & 2
1 When Jesus had spoken these words, he went forth with his disciples over the brook Cedron, where was a garden, into the which he entered, and his disciples.
2 And Judas also, which betrayed him, knew the place: for Jesus ofttimes resorted thither with his disciples.

Keep your prayer life a personal thing between you and God.

Pray to Him in secret; make a note of your prayers (mentally or otherwise) and indicate when God answers.

Matthew 6:5 & 6
5 And when thou prayest, thou shalt not be as the hypocrites are: for they love to pray standing in the synagogues and

in the corners of the streets, that they may be seen of men. Verily I say unto you, They have their reward.
6 But thou, when thou prayest, enter into thy closet, and when thou hast shut thy door, pray to thy Father which is in secret; and thy Father which seeth in secret shall reward thee openly.

Use simple language and terms you know.

As you grow your will learn from others, but learn to separate the style from the substance. God knows what you need before you ask Him, so use language that you understand.

Matthew 6:7 & 8
7 But when ye pray, use not vain repetitions, as the heathen do: for they think that they shall be heard for their much speaking.
8 Be not ye therefore like unto them: for your Father knoweth what things ye have need of, before ye ask him.

Pray in the name of Jesus.

Use the name that heaven recognizes and as you do you will also be following Jesus' instruction.

John 14:13 & 14
13 And whatsoever ye shall ask in my name, that will I do, that the Father may be glorified in the Son.
14 If ye shall ask any thing in my name, I will do it.

Pray in faith and believe.

This may surprise you but there are a whole lot people praying who do not believe they will receive the things for which they prayed. There is a passage in Acts 12 where the saints were praying for the Apostle Peter because he was imprisoned. God answered the prayer and released Peter and he came by the prayer meeting; but the saints did not believe a word of it. When someone insisted it was Peter, here is what happened:

Acts 12:15 & 16
15 And they said unto her, Thou art mad. But she constantly affirmed that it was even so. Then said they, It is his angel.
16 But Peter continued knocking: and when they had opened the door, and saw him, they were astonished.

So friend, when you pray, believe that God will answer your prayer. Leave the timing up to Him though. He may answer right away or some time later, but He will answer.

Mark 11:22 - 24
22 And Jesus answering saith unto them, Have faith in God.
23 For verily I say unto you, That whosoever shall say unto this mountain, Be thou removed, and be thou cast into the sea; and shall not doubt in his heart, but shall believe that those things which he saith shall come to pass; he shall have whatsoever he saith.
24 Therefore I say unto you, What things soever ye desire, when ye pray, believe that ye receive them, and ye shall have them.

Ask according to the will of God.

It is useless to ask for something that is not in His will for you to have. After all, He knows what is best for you.

1 John 5:14 & 15
14 And this is the confidence that we have in him, that, if we ask any thing according to his will, he heareth us:
15 And if we know that he hear us, whatsoever we ask, we know that we have the petitions that we desired of him.

Persist in prayer.

Please read the parables that Jesus gave in Luke 18:1 – 8. In it you will find that a persistent woman convinced an unjust judge to work on her behalf because of her constant nagging. Jesus pointed out that He is much more willing than that unjust judge, to respond to our prayers.

Matthew 7:7
Ask, and it shall be given you; seek, and ye shall find; knock, and it shall be opened unto you:

Luke 18:1
And he spake a parable unto them to this end, that men ought always to pray, and not to faint;

1 Thessalonians 5:17
Pray without ceasing.

Develop and maintain good fruits, that is, fruit of the Spirit.

Good fruits come as you trust in the Lord, yield yourself to Him and obey His Word. God will hear those who hear Him.

John 15:16
Ye have not chosen me, but I have chosen you, and ordained you, that ye should go and bring forth fruit, and that your fruit should remain: that whatsoever ye shall ask of the Father in my name, he may give it you.

Come to God humbly.

Please read the parable Jesus gave in Luke 18:9-14 about the Publican and a Pharisee. According to 2 Chronicles 7:14, God promised to hear us if we humble ourselves and pray.

Pray about everything, worry about nothing.

Many people do not regard 'worry' as a sin. But we are command to trust and not worry, so to worry is to go contrary to the council of God.

Philippians 4:6 & 7
6 Be careful for nothing; but in every thing by prayer and supplication with thanksgiving let your requests be made known unto God.
7 And the peace of God, which passeth all understanding, shall keep your hearts and minds through Christ Jesus.

HINDRANCES TO PRAYER

God does not hear the prayer of a sinful heart unless the person is confessing and repenting.

Psalm 51:17
The sacrifices of God are a broken spirit: a broken and a contrite heart, O God, thou wilt not despise.

Psalm 66:18
If I regard iniquity in my heart, the Lord will not hear me:

If we do not pray in faith our prayers will not be answered because faith pleases God (Hebrews 11:6).

Romans 14:23
And he that doubteth is damned if he eat, because he eateth not of faith: for whatsoever is not of faith is sin.

James 1:6 & 7
6 But let him ask in faith, nothing wavering. For he that wavereth is like a wave of the sea driven with the wind and tossed.

7 For let not that man think that he shall receive any thing of the Lord.

God does not respond to prayers that are accompanied with wrong motives.

James 4:3
Ye ask, and receive not, because ye ask amiss, that ye may consume it upon your lusts.

Men who dishonour their wives do not receive answers to their prayers.

1 Peter 3:7
Likewise, ye husbands, dwell with them according to knowledge, giving honour unto the wife, as unto the weaker vessel, and as being heirs together of the grace of life; that your prayers be not hindered.

CHAPTER TWENTY FOUR

FASTING AND BIBLE STUDY

The Word of God encourages the believer to pray and fast. In general, fasting is simply the abstinence from food. It has benefits not only for the soul and spirit but also for the body. Here are some Biblical benefits of fasting:

- **Fasting looses the bands of wickedness and liberates captives**

Isaiah 58:6
Is not this the fast that I have chosen? to loose the bands of wickedness, to undo the heavy burdens, and to let the oppressed go free, and that ye break every yoke?

- **Fasting gives power over stubborn demons**

Mark 9:29
And he said unto them, This kind can come forth by nothing, but by prayer and fasting.

- **Fasting makes you mighty in the Spirit**

Luke 4:1 – 2 & 14
1 And Jesus being full of the Holy Ghost returned from Jordan, and was led by the Spirit into the wilderness,
2 Being forty days tempted of the devil. And in those days he did eat nothing: and when they were ended, he afterward hungered.

14 And Jesus returned in the power of the Spirit into Galilee: and there went out a fame of him through all the region round about.

- **Fasting gets you an answer from God**

Acts 10:30
And Cornelius said, Four days ago I was fasting until this hour; and at the ninth hour I prayed in my house, and, behold, a man stood before me in bright clothing,

- **Fasting gives us more control over our flesh (self-control) and it is a sure way of denying the flesh** (Colossians 3:5).

Romans 8:13
For if ye live after the flesh, ye shall die: but if ye through the Spirit do mortify the deeds of the body, ye shall live.

- **Fasting intensifies the mission and prepares those whom are called.**

Acts 14:23
And when they had ordained them elders in every church, and had prayed with fasting, they commended them to the Lord, on whom they believed.

Types of Fasts

Throughout the Scriptures you will find that there were at least three types of fasts.

Daniel's Fast or Self-denial

In the book of Daniel you will read about this type of fast. Daniel refused to eat the king's meat, but settled instead for a different diet, one that was less than the normal.

Daniel 1:8 & 12
8 But Daniel purposed in his heart that he would not defile himself with the portion of the king's meat, nor with the wine which he drank: therefore he requested of the prince of the eunuchs that he might not defile himself.

12 Prove thy servants, I beseech thee, ten days; and let them give us pulse to eat, and water to drink.

Day's or Partial Fast

This type of fast lasts for twelve hours at the most. It starts at sunrise and is broken at sunset. In this case it is possible to go without food or water for the entire period.

Judges 20:26
Then all the children of Israel, and all the people, went up, and came unto the house of God, and wept, and sat there before the Lord, and fasted that day until even, and offered burnt offerings and peace offerings before the Lord.

1 Samuel 14:24
And the men of Israel were distressed that day: for Saul had adjured the people, saying, Cursed be the man that eateth any food until evening, that I may be avenged on mine enemies. So none of the people tasted any food.

Absolute or Complete Fast

This fast lasts for a complete cycle. The candidate would eat absolutely nothing for the term of the fast. However, water is usually taken if the fast lasts for more than three days. Please note that after Jesus' forty-day fast, He was not thirsty, only hungry.

Esther 4:16
Go, gather together all the Jews that are present in Shushan, and fast ye for me, and neither eat nor drink three days, night or day: I also and my maidens will fast likewise; and so will I go in unto the king, which is not according to the law: and if I perish, I perish.

Matthew 4:2
And when he had fasted forty days and forty nights, he was afterward an hungred.

How to do a proper Fast

1. Prepare yourself mentally, spiritually and physically. This is especially true if you intend to go on a long fast. Begin the same number of days before the fast as the days of actual fasting to slowly adjust your body to less food.
2. If you will be fasting for more than 3 days drink water to keep the bodily functions working.
3. When breaking your fast slowly graduate your stomach from light soups to regular food as eating too much too early can severely damage you shrunken stomach.
4. Keep your fasting personal and private.

Matthew 6:16 - 18
16 Moreover when ye fast, be not, as the hypocrites, of a sad countenance: for they disfigure their faces, that they may appear unto men to fast...
17 But thou, when thou fastest, anoint thine head, and wash thy face;

18 That thou appear not unto men to fast, but unto thy Father which is in secret: and thy Father, which seeth in secret, shall reward thee openly.

5. Avoid strenuous activities or excessive walking while on a long fast.

Mark 8:2 & 3
2 I have compassion on the multitude, because they have now been with me three days, and have nothing to eat:
3 And if I send them away fasting to their own houses, they will faint by the way: for divers of them came from far.

6. Expect some physical side effects (headache, cramps, etc) at the onset.

The Psalmist David encountered a couple of them during his fast.

Psalm 109:24
My knees are weak through fasting; and my flesh faileth of fatness.

Hunger pangs or a headache may try to dissuade you from fasting, but pray and read your Bible every chance you get. It is said that, unless accompanied by prayer and the Word, going without food is simply a hunger strike and not a real fast.

Deuteronomy 8:3
And he humbled thee, and suffered thee to hunger, and fed thee with manna, which thou knewest not, neither did thy fathers know; that he might make thee know that man doth not live by bread only, but by every word that proceedeth out of the mouth of the Lord doth man live.

In conclusion, the Bible encourages us all to pray and fast; no one is exempted.

1 Timothy 2:8
I will therefore that men pray every where, lifting up holy hands, without wrath and doubting.

While Jesus walked the earth the disciples were exempted from fasting, but He said that in His physical absence they should fast.

Matthew 9:15
And Jesus said unto them, Can the children of the bride-chamber mourn, as long as the bridegroom is with them? but the days will come, when the bridegroom shall be taken from them, and then shall they fast.

When a Church prays and fasts together the corporate results are astounding (Joel 2:15 – 32).

2 Chronicles 7:14
If my people, which are called by my name, shall humble themselves, and pray, and seek my face, and turn from their wicked ways; then will I hear from heaven, and will forgive their sin, and will heal their land.

Please note: To humble oneself also means, 'to fast'.

Psalm 35:13
But as for me, when they were sick, my clothing was sack-cloth: I humbled my soul with fasting; and my prayer returned into mine own bosom.

Prayer and fasting should precede the selection and appointment of officers in any Church.

- **Jesus spent a night in prayer before selecting the Apostles**

Luke 6:12 & 13
12 And it came to pass in those days, that he went out into a mountain to pray, and continued all night in prayer to God.
13 And when it was day, he called unto him his disciples: and of them he chose twelve, whom also he named apostles;

- **Other examples from the Early Church**

Acts 13:2
As they ministered to the Lord, and fasted, the Holy Ghost said, Separate me Barnabas and Saul for the work where-unto I have called them.

Bible Study

Every newborn baby requires food to grow and survive. A believer in Christ is no different. It is in the Word of God that you will find the spiritual nutrients necessary for your constant spiritual growth and development.

Luke 4:4
And Jesus answered him, saying, It is written, That man shall not live by bread alone, but by every word of God.

1 Peter 2:2
As newborn babes, desire the sincere milk of the word, that ye may grow thereby:

Set aside a time to study the Word of God.

You should do this daily, either alone, or with someone who can guide you correctly. Be sure to ask the Holy Spirit for illumination (1 Corinthians 2:14). You could start by praying the Words found in Psalm 119:18 given at the beginning of this book.

Acts 8:30 & 31
30 And Philip ran thither to him, and heard him read the prophet Esaias, and said, Understandest thou what thou readest?
31 And he said, How can I, except some man should guide me? And he desired Philip that he would come up and sit with him.

2 Timothy 2:15
Study to shew thyself approved unto God, a workman that needeth not to be ashamed, rightly dividing the word of truth.

1 John 2:27
But the anointing which ye have received of him abideth in you, and ye need not that any man teach you: but as the same anointing teacheth you of all things, and is truth, and is no lie, and even as it hath taught you, ye shall abide in him.

Practice what the Word of God teaches

Nothing gets the job done like doing the job. Work works! Learn to implement what you learn. Let the Word work in your heart and life.

Joshua 1:8
This book of the law shall not depart out of thy mouth; but thou shalt meditate therein day and night, that thou mayest observe to do according to all that is written therein: for then thou shalt make thy way prosperous, and then thou shalt have good success.

James 1:22
But be ye doers of the word, and not hearers only, deceiving your own selves.

Compare what you learn with the Word

The entire Christian experience is characterized by what is taught in the Word of God. If you cannot find it in the Word of God, question it.

John 5:39
Search the scriptures; for in them ye think ye have eternal life: and they are they which testify of me.

Acts 17:11 & 12
11 These were more noble than those in Thessalonica, in that they received the word with all readiness of mind, and searched the scriptures daily, whether those things were so.
12 Therefore many of them believed; also of honourable women which were Greeks, and of men, not a few.

Galatians 1:8 & 9
8 But though we, or an angel from heaven, preach any other gospel unto you than that which we have preached unto you, let him be accursed.
9 As we said before, so say I now again, If any man preach any other gospel unto you than that ye have received, let him be accursed.

Life is in the Word

The Scriptures will teach you how to live a victorious Christian life. Remember that the Bible is like a lamp (Psalm 119:105). The closer we get to the light, the more we see things we could not see before.

Psalm 119:130
The entrance of thy words giveth light; it giveth under-standing unto the simple.

Meditate on the Word of God

Take a few extra moments and think on what you have read from the Bible and you will have peace and blessing in your life.

Psalm 1:1 & 2
1 Blessed is the man that walketh not in the counsel of the ungodly, nor standeth in the way of sinners, nor sitteth in the seat of the scornful.
2 But his delight is in the law of the Lord; and in his law doth he meditate day and night.

Psalm 19:14
Let the words of my mouth, and the meditation of my heart, be acceptable in thy sight, O Lord, my strength, and my redeemer.

The bottom line is that you have no more of God than you do of His Word. He is the Word (John 1:1 and Revelation 19:13).

1 Samuel 3:21
And the Lord appeared again in Shiloh: for the Lord revealed himself to Samuel in Shiloh by the word of the Lord.

CHAPTER TWENTY FIVE

THE CHURCH

The Church is the community of believers that fellowship and worship God together in spirit and in truth.

When we are born again, we are automatically placed in the family of God. God ensures we are cared for, nourished and taught His Word and Will through the Church. This local body is very important and although most people have a general idea of what is meant when they hear the word, 'church', it is needful that we emphasize certain points.

The Church belongs to God.

God has given many great leaders the privilege of pasturing His flock, but the sheep belong to God.

Psalm 100:3
Know ye that the Lord he is God: it is he that hath made us, and not we ourselves; we are his people, and the sheep of his pasture.

Matthew 16:18
And I say also unto thee, That thou art Peter, and upon this rock I will build my church; and the gates of hell shall not prevail against it.

Acts 20:28
Take heed therefore unto yourselves, and to all the flock, over the which the Holy Ghost hath made you overseers, to feed the church of God, which he hath purchased with his own blood.

The Church of God is attractive.

The Church has had its share of trouble. History has lots to say about the persecutions and tribulations that have been heaped upon her. Yet even during her darkest days many have come to her seeking refuge.

Luke 16:16
The law and the prophets were until John: since that time the kingdom of God is preached, and every man presseth into it.

John 12:19
The Pharisees therefore said among themselves, Perceive ye how ye prevail nothing? behold, the world is gone after him.

The Church echoes the voice of Christ and invites all to come.

The supreme task of the Church is the evangelization of the world. Through missionary outreach at home and abroad and through various other innovative ministries the Church has been successful in proclaiming the gospel of Jesus Christ to the entire world.

Matthew 11:28
Come unto me, all ye that labour and are heavy laden, and I will give you rest.

John 3:16
For God so loved the world, that he gave his only begotten
Son, that whosoever believeth in him should not perish, but
have everlasting life.

Revelation 22:17
And the Spirit and the bride say, Come. And let him that
heareth say, Come. And let him that is athirst come. And
whosoever will, let him take the water of life freely.

The Church is universal.

The Church is not confined to any one nationality, culture or race
or even a building. Jesus Christ gave His life for the whole world.
Although several religious groups would love to claim Him as their
very own; the Lord Jesus will not be owned by any.

John 2:24 & 25
24 But Jesus did not commit himself unto them, because he
knew all men,
25 And needed not that any should testify of man: for he
knew what was in man.

Salvation is not a denomination, and no one should reject the
plan of salvation for fear of being labeled a member of any particular group.

Acts 10:35
But in every nation he that feareth him, and worketh righ-
teousness, is accepted with him.

Romans 10:12
For there is no difference between the Jew and the Greek: for
the same Lord over all is rich unto all that call upon him.

Revelation 5:9
And they sung a new song, saying, Thou art worthy to take the book, and to open the seals thereof: for thou wast slain, and hast redeemed us to God by thy blood out of every kindred, and tongue, and people, and nation;

The Church is in the congregation.

The people or congregation constitutes the church and yet, not all the people in the congregation are in the Church. Perhaps it would be better to say that the Church is in the congregation. To be absolutely clear, the Church is that called out group of people who have surrendered their lives and have decided to follow God through His Word.

John 13:10
Jesus saith to him, He that is washed needeth not save to wash his feet, but is clean every whit: and ye are clean, but not all.

Romans 9:6
... For they are not all Israel, which are of Israel:

The Church is not a building.

There certainly are a lot of beautiful edifices around; some loaded with the latest technological gadgets, innovative designs and state-of-the-art equipment. But though we need a building for many obvious reasons, the Church really comprises the saints. If need be, we can have a 'church' without a building.

1 Corinthians 3:9
For we are labourers together with God: ye are God's husbandry, ye are God's building.

1 Peter 2:5
Ye also, as lively stones, are built up a spiritual house, an holy priesthood, to offer up spiritual sacrifices, acceptable to God by Jesus Christ.

The Church is victorious.

Since the inception of the Church many tyrants have tried to wipe it out with the very blood of those who are in it; yet it still stands. Remember what Jesus said about His Church in Matthew 16:18? He said, *"...the gates of hell shall not prevail against it."*

John 10:28
And I give unto them eternal life; and they shall never perish, neither shall any man pluck them out of my hand.

Acts 19:20
So mightily grew the word of God and prevailed.

The Church is alive.

As a living organism, the Church is expected to grow and develop. Each member is gifted in a unique way and their best contributions in every way will certainly increase the body of Christ as a whole.

Ephesians 4:16
From whom the whole body fitly joined together and compacted by that which every joint supplieth, according to the effectual working in the measure of every part, maketh increase of the body unto the edifying of itself in love.

THE STRUCTURE OF THE CHURCH

The Church is synonymous to a natural body, and like the body, the Church has many members. Not all the members are alike, but they work together to ensure the function and purpose of the Church is realized.

Romans 12:4
For as we have many members in one body, and all members have not the same office:

1 Corinthians 12:12
For as the body is one, and hath many members, and all the members of that one body, being many, are one body: so also is Christ.

1 Corinthians 12:20
But now are they many members, yet but one body.

The Head of the Church is the Lord Jesus Christ.

Every body has a head and Christ is the Head of the church (the body of Christ) and without the head, the body is dead.

Ephesians 4:15
But speaking the truth in love, may grow up into him in all things, which is the head, even Christ:

Ephesians 5:23
For the husband is the head of the wife, even as Christ is the head of the church: and he is the saviour of the body.

Colossians 1:18
And he is the head of the body, the church: who is the beginning, the firstborn from the dead; that in all things he might have the preeminence.

The members of the Church make up the rest of the body.

For a complete view of the body of Christ you can study 1 Corinthians 12:12–27.

Romans 12:4 & 5
4 For as we have many members in one body, and all
members have not the same office:
5 So we, being many, are one body in Christ, and every one
members one of another.

Ephesians 2:20 & 21
21 And are built upon the foundation of the apostles and
prophets, Jesus Christ himself being the chief corner stone;
21 In whom all the building fitly framed together groweth
unto an holy temple in the Lord:

Order in the Church

We have already seen that God gives spiritual gifts which enable
the body of Christ in the ministry He has entrusted to us. However,
God also gives a people as gifts to the body of Christ. These person-
gifts are mentioned in the Word of God along with the purpose they
serve.

Ephesians 4:11 - 14
11 And he gave some, apostles; and some, prophets; and
some, evangelists; and some, pastors and teachers;
12 For the perfecting of the saints, for the work of the
ministry, for the edifying of the body of Christ:
13 Till we all come in the unity of the faith, and of the knowl-
edge of the Son of God, unto a perfect man, unto the measure
of the stature of the fulness of Christ:
14 That we henceforth be no more children, tossed to and
fro, and carried about with every wind of doctrine, by the
sleight of men, and cunning craftiness, whereby they lie in
wait to deceive;

Therefore, your pastor is a gift to you and to the local church
where he or she serves the Lord. However, he or she has to be called
by God to be a pastor. In other words, God will only send (give)
those He has called.

1 Corinthians 7:20
Let every man abide in the same calling wherein he was called.

- **Honour those who are your leaders.**

The Bible instructs us to care for and respect those that labour among us. In other words, care for the gifts that God has given unto us.

1 Thessalonians 5:12 & 13
12 And we beseech you, brethren, to know them which labour among you, and are over you in the Lord, and admonish you;
13 And to esteem them very highly in love for their work's sake. And be at peace among yourselves.

1 Timothy 5:17
Let the elders that rule well be counted worthy of double honour, especially they who labour in the word and doctrine.

Hebrews 13:17
Obey them that have the rule over you, and submit your-selves: for they watch for your souls, as they that must give account, that they may do it with joy, and not with grief: for that is unprofitable for you.

Church Check Up

Are you in the Church, or do you just go to church? It is great to shake the preachers hand and have your name on a church roll, but is your name also written in the Lamb's book of life?

Revelations 20:15
And whosoever was not found written in the book of life was cast into the lake of fire.

I know people who have given their lives to help other people; serving as missionaries in the most remote parts of the Earth. Yet good works alone is not enough. Jesus does not know us by our good works.

Matthew 7:21 & 23
21 Not every one that saith unto me, Lord, Lord, shall enter into the kingdom of heaven; but he that doeth the will of my Father which is in heaven.
22 Many will say to me in that day, Lord, Lord, have we not prophesied in thy name? and in thy name have cast out devils? and in thy name done many wonderful works?
23 And then will I profess unto them, I never knew you: depart from me, ye that work iniquity.

Names Given to the Church

The Church is known by various names today; First Apostolic Seventh Day Church of God of the Open Bible Baptist Episcopal Ministry. This is mainly so because of denominational lines. Others have moved away from denominational titles and have opted for a 'Community Church', Family Life Centre' or something a little less "offensive".

The Bible has some names given to the Church and this is simply for information reasons only. I am in no way, shape or form, implying that you should only attend a church which goes by one of those scriptural names. Any group can go by any name they choose to use, but their deeds and speech will eventually reveal who they really are.

- The body of Christ (Romans 12:5)
- The Lamb's wife (Revelations 21:9)
- The church of God (Acts 20:28, 1 Corinthians 1:2; 10:32; 11:22; 15:9; 2 Corinthians 1:1, Galatians 1:13 & 1 Timothy 3:5 & 15)
- The general assembly & church of the firstborn (Hebrews 12:23)

- God's husbandry and Building (1 Corinthians 3:9)
- The house & household of God (Ephesians 2:19; 1 Timothy 3:15; Hebrews 10:21 and 1 Peter 4:17)
- The pillar and ground of the truth (1 Timothy 3:15)
- A spiritual house (1 Peter 2:5)
- Temple of God (1 Corinthians 3:16; 1 Corinthians 6:19; 2 Corinthians 6:16 and Ephesians 2:20 – 22)

CHAPTER TWENTY SIX

YOU AND YOUR LOCAL CHURCH

Each local church may have a different manner of operation and administration than another church. However, each believer has certain responsibilities to the local church congregation that he/she is required to fulfill and these can be done without an official title. Official titles have their place, but the thing which I am about to describe should be observed with or without a title.

You are a Light Bearer

Each believer is required to give a good representation of the Lord and of his Church. We are light bearers while the world lies in darkness.

Matthew 5:14 - 16
14 Ye are the light of the world. A city that is set on an hill cannot be hid.
15 Neither do men light a candle, and put it under a bushel, but on a candlestick; and it giveth light unto all that are in the house.
16 Let your light so shine before men, that they may see your good works, and glorify your Father which is in heaven.

Philippians. 2:14 - 16
14 Do all things without murmurings and disputings:
15 That ye may be blameless and harmless, the sons of God,
without rebuke, in the midst of a crooked and perverse nation,
among whom ye shine as lights in the world;
16 Holding forth the word of life; that I may rejoice in the
day of Christ, that I have not run in vain, neither laboured
in vain.

Be a Godly Example

The Scriptures even say we are living epistles. Our lives are the only Word many will see. Let us live in such a way that our actions testify of God's love.

John 13:15
For I have given you an example, that ye should do as I have
done to you.

2 Corinthians 3:2
Ye are our epistle written in our hearts, known and read of
all men:

1 Timothy 4:12
Let no man despise thy youth; but be thou an example of the
believers, in word, in conversation, in charity, in spirit, in
faith, in purity.

Live a Sanctified Life

The word sanctified means set apart from one thing but placed unto another. Believers in Christ must live a sanctified life every day. We need to put on righteousness every day and try to be consistent in our Christian walk. This goes beyond just being an example; every believer wants to ready when Jesus comes and no one knows exactly when that will be.

1 Kings 18:21
And Elijah came unto all the people, and said, How long halt ye between two opinions? if the Lord be God, follow him: but if Baal, then follow him. And the people answered him not a word.

Titus 2:11 & 12
11 For the grace of God that bringeth salvation hath appeared to all men,
12 Teaching us that, denying ungodliness and worldly lusts, we should live soberly, righteously, and godly, in this present world;

Revelation 3:15 & 16
15 I know thy works, that thou art neither cold nor hot: I would thou wert cold or hot.
16 So then because thou art lukewarm, and neither cold nor hot, I will spue thee out of my mouth.

We live a life that is pleasing unto the Lord by staying away from sin. God wants us to have fellowship with Him; to be able to come into His presence and worship Him. When sin is in our lives, we are hindered by the holy nature of God.

Leviticus 20:7
Sanctify yourselves therefore, and be ye holy: for I am the Lord your God.

So God by His Holy Spirit comes and abides in the life of all His children because we are sons of God, and by doing so, He enables us to live a holy life.

Romans 8:9
But ye are not in the flesh, but in the Spirit, if so be that the Spirit of God dwell in you. Now if any man have not the Spirit of Christ, he is none of his.

HOW TO LIVE A SANCTIFIED LIFE

Sanctification is a process. The more we yield to God, dropping off sins as He reveals them to us, consecrating our lives to Him, it is the more sanctified we become. It is not an overnight thing. Many of the saints you may admire today certainly did not attain their level of holiness overnight. They have been walking with God for some time and have learned to yield to His Word and change their lives accordingly.

The Word of God and the faith it produces sanctify us. (Romans 10:17).

John 17:17
Sanctify them through thy truth: thy word is truth.

Acts 26:18
To open their eyes, and to turn them from darkness to light, and from the power of Satan unto God, that they may receive forgiveness of sins, and inheritance among them which are sanctified by faith that is in me.

The Holy Ghost sanctifies.

Romans 15:16
That I should be the minister of Jesus Christ to the Gentiles, ministering the gospel of God, that the offering up of the Gentiles might be acceptable, being sanctified by the Holy Ghost.

Sanctification also comes through prayer.

1 Timothy 4:5
For it is sanctified by the word of God and prayer.

The Blood of Jesus sanctifies us.

Hebrews 13:12
Wherefore Jesus also, that he might sanctify the people with his own blood, suffered without the gate.

The Father sanctifies us and Christ preserves us.

Jude 1:1
Jude, the servant of Jesus Christ, and brother of James, to them that are sanctified by God the Father, and preserved in Jesus Christ, and called:

CHURCH ATTENDANCE

We live in a busy world, and we are fortunate to have the Word of God in various computerized forms and gadgets, being preached and taught through various media. Many ministries can be viewed on demand over the internet or several times per day on cable television. However, there is still a need to belong to a local church.

Hebrews 10:25
Not forsaking the assembling of ourselves together, as the manner of some is; but exhorting one another: and so much the more, as ye see the day approaching.

Your regular meal comes from home, your local Church.

We live in a mega time; mega churches and mega conferences. However, what you get from those gatherings are like vitamins. They supplement what you get from your local church. There is no way you could possibly survive going from conference to conference. The local church is there to cater to your spiritual growth and to encourage fellowship and discipline.

Acts 20:7
And upon the first day of the week, when the disciples came together to break bread, Paul preached unto them, ready to depart on the morrow; and continued his speech until midnight.

2 Thessalonians 3:14
And if any man obey not our word by this epistle, note that man, and have no company with him, that he may be ashamed.

Our financial obligation is better managed though the local church.

The income generated by the freewill offerings and tithes allows the church to fulfill its financial obligations and carry on its daily operations meeting the needs of the community.

1 Corinthians 16:2
Upon the first day of the week let every one of you lay by him in store, as God hath prospered him, that there be no gatherings when I come.

Individuals discover their God-given gifts and talents in the local Church.

It is in the local church that we grow, learn Christ, and are strengthened through regular fellowship and corporate worship.

Colossians 3:16
Let the word of Christ dwell in you richly in all wisdom; teaching and admonishing one another in psalms and hymns and spiritual songs, singing with grace in your hearts to the Lord.

FINANCIAL SUPPORT

The Church is in the business of saving and preparing souls for the second coming of the Lord Jesus Christ. It is not a profit making entity where making money and satisfying shareholders are concerned. But you and I know that money is needed to transact any business on earth and to provide for the various needs of the people and ministries of the church.

For example, the saints need a comfortable place in which to worship the Lord Jesus, and must therefore be able to pay the bills that come with owning and operating such a place. It is through the faithful financial support of the saints that the Church is able to do this.

God blesses the children of God to get wealth.

Deuteronomy 8:18
But thou shalt remember the Lord thy God: for it is he that giveth thee power to get wealth, that he may establish his covenant which he sware unto thy fathers, as it is this day.

God requires a tenth (or tithe).

Genesis 28:22
And this stone, which I have set for a pillar, shall be God's house: and of all that thou shalt give me I will surely give the tenth unto thee.

Malachi 3:10
Bring ye all the tithes into the storehouse, that there may be meat in mine house, and prove me now herewith, saith the Lord of hosts, if I will not open you the windows of heaven, and pour you out a blessing, that there shall not be room enough to receive it.

WITNESSING AND SOUL WINNING

The Church is a living organism. It grows numerically one member at a time. Each of us has been empowered by the Holy Ghost to witness to others (Acts 1:8), and share with them the love of Christ.

Acts 2:47
Praising God, and having favour with all the people. And the Lord added to the church daily such as should be saved.

We can be effective witnesses in the following ways.

By loving one another

Love is more than a feeling. It is manifested in our actions and reactions. God has placed His love in each of us and we ought to allow Him to love others through us.

John 13:35
By this shall all men know that ye are my disciples, if ye have love one to another.

1 John 3:16
Hereby perceive we the love of God, because he laid down his life for us: and we ought to lay down our lives for the brethren.

By your lifestyle, others are watching you

This is not to say we live our lives to please people. Certainly, our actions should first be pleasing to God. But as good witnesses we need to ensure that we do not give others any reasons to reject the God we serve. Some people seem to always get the wrong impression no matter what you do, but special effort and consideration should be given to ensure that what we know on the inside is reflected in what we do.

Sure, God knows your heart. But you are not witnessing to God but to people and people cannot see your heart; "...*for man looketh on the outward appearance, but the LORD looketh on the heart...*" (1 Samuels 16:7).

Matthew 5:16
Let your light so shine before men, that they may see your good works, and glorify your Father which is in heaven.

Ephesians 5:15
See then that ye walk circumspectly, not as fools, but as wise,

By your speech

Your testimony (telling others what Christ has done for you) is one of the most effective forms of witnessing. Many believers choose to witness only by what others see in them, rather than deliberately capitalizing on an opportunity to verbally share their faith. As a result, they place more emphasis on their appearance instead of their speech.

I admit; it is not easy to witness to others; especially in a world that seems more tolerant to everything else but God. But many of us find ways to do difficult things. As we put the matter before God daily He will provide opportunities and may even start the conversations for us. We then must be ready to follow through on His leading.

Titus 2:8
Sound speech, that cannot be condemned; that he that is of the contrary part may be ashamed, having no evil thing to say of you.

2 Timothy 4:2
Preach the word; be instant in season, out of season; reprove, rebuke, exhort with all longsuffering and doctrine.

Printed in the United States
138712LV00002B/2/P